I WAS MAN'S TRASH,
now i'm in the
KING'S TREASURE

I WAS MAN'S TRASH, now i'm in the KING'S TREASURE

GEORGIA SMITH

I Was Man's Trash, Now I'm in the King's Treasury

Copyright © 2024 by Georgia Smith. All rights reserved.

No part of this publication may be reproduced, stored in a retrieval system or transmitted in any way by any means, electronic, mechanical, photocopy, recording or otherwise without the prior permission of the author except as provided by USA copyright law.

The opinions expressed by the author are not necessarily those of URLink Print and Media.

1603 Capitol Ave., Suite 310 Cheyenne, Wyoming USA 82001
1-888-980-6523 | admin@urlinkpublishing.com

URLink Print and Media is committed to excellence in the publishing industry.

Book design copyright © 2024 by URLink Print and Media. All rights reserved.

Published in the United States of America

Library of Congress Control Number: 2024923957
ISBN 978-1-68486-981-7 (Paperback)
ISBN 978-1-68486-982-4 (Digital)

02.10.24

I Was Man's Trash, Now I'm in the King's Treasury is about a woman writing to her daughter, Tee, who wanted to know about her mother's life, and to any other daughters and sons that have been hurt or devastated in life no matter how old or young you maybe. You may also be the one that has caused the pain to others, but you too can receive the free gift of no condemnation. All though this is a story about my life and my choices, as you read this, please remember that it is never too late to change your future. This is not meant to be a sad story but one of victory. I wrote this book not to point a finger at anyone. It is my hope that some would be healed while reading the pages of this book. I want you to know that when you have an understanding that God loves you and is for you and not against you and that you have been forgiven, you are also able to forgive those that have harmed you. Where men literally walked on me, stepped over me, and threw me aside as trash, the King of kings saw me, picked me up, cleaned and polished me, and declared me to be a valuable jewel.

The story is set in a small poor town in California where there should be plenty of food for everyone in the Golden State and not just for the limited few. Here, most everyone pulls together with what little help they can give to each other, but when three young girls lose the necessary help and guidance of a mother, things are turned upside down.

CHAPTER

1

We live in different cultures and in different places in the world, and when we are harmed by any person whether knowingly or unknowingly, or any circumstance in our life, the truth is only God can heal us. Yes, there are times that you may need to go have counsel; but in the end, they can only do so much because Living Life is real, it is not a fiction book.

For some reason, when we get older, we begin to look for our roots—little pieces of a puzzle that make us who we are or something or someone that we can connect with to contribute to the reason we do what we do in our life. Things that we have pushed to the back of our minds into the farthermost crevices and voids will began to sneak back out. No matter how we have tried to lock them away. I have found that locking them away only prolongs the healing process.

They will find their way out in other issues. There will come a time in our lives that we want to know just what we are here on this earth for, and how the things that have happened in our lives have changed our futures or will direct us to our future. It's a little like the salmon fish that has a sense of home built in them that causes them to return where they were born to lay their eggs or the migrating birds to sense when it is time to fly south for the winter.

I decided to go on an adventure to see if I could find some sort of connection from my past to the person that I am today. So where should I start? It was really God's doing that I was able to trace a few relatives in Mississippi. My husband and I had had a craving for barbeque one weekend a few weeks before we were going to leave on our trip, and I decided to go to one of the few locations that sold it in our town. While I was waiting for my order, another man came in, and we started talking about how much easier it was to find barbeque in the South than in California. I introduced myself as Marie, and he said his was Calvin. The next thing I knew, we discovered that we both had family in Collins, Mississippi. He thought that his aunt was married to one of my relatives. He gave me a phone number to call, the phone number of someone in town here that might know the number of the person in Collins; and sure enough, when I called it—it seemed that we were related. It turned out that the people that I called weren't related to me at all, but did know some of my cousins that lived in Collins and gave me their number. I called to Collins, Mississippi, and spoke to one of my cousins that I had never even heard of before. We set up a meeting time on our trip to get together.

Okay, so I was excited to get this journey started so that I could meet some of my relatives and see some of the places that my mom and dad had been in their youths. We went to my husband's family reunion first, which was an encounter all by itself, if I may add. There was what seemed like a thousand people waiting for us to arrive when we drove up at Lou's grandmother, Grand-Hollingsworth's place, although it was only about 120 people, which was just as bad. Starkville is comprised of woods, country, and more woods. Most of the people have acres and acres of land, which was no different with Lou's grandmother's place. When Lou left, he was still a young child, and everyone wanted to adopt him because his mother was ill at the time and could not raise him. One of his younger aunts kidnapped him and took him home with her to live in Chicago. She raised him until he became a teenager. Now everyone wanted to see whom he had married. Can you imagine stepping out of a car with over a hundred strangers' pairs of eyes watching to see what you look like.

One of his female cousins was the first to run up and whisk him off, leaving me standing there not knowing anyone. It was a cousin who had called our house, asking to speak with Lou without even speaking to me. I finally had a woman-to-woman with her; she apologized for her behavior, and later we became friends. It was so hot when we got out of the air-conditioned car that it was somewhat hard to breathe. While I was still struggling with the heat, different ones of Lou's aunts came up and introduced themselves to me. Lou's aunt that had partially raised him. His brother Jerry and his wife were there. I had met all three of them a few years earlier when we went to Chicago; knowing them helped me to feel a little more comfortable. Lou and his cousin came waltzing back up after about a half hour, just when everyone had started lining up to eat from what seemed like a mile-long smorgasbord. After everyone was filled with every Southern fare you could name, we were all sitting around outside when the interrogation began. They all wanted to know what California was like. How did we survive the earthquakes? Is everyone in California rich? Have we seen any movie stars. We tried to explain that the earthquakes weren't all over California, and if they did have one, most of the time you wouldn't know it. We told them that the movie stars were in Los Angeles and not very many in Northern California. The next morning it rained, and I literally thought that I was going to die. I had never experienced the humidity in that part of the country. After the rain, the air was so heavy that I could hardly breathe. I went inside of Lou's grandmother's house and lay down on the bed in the guest room that we used. I waited to die. I didn't believe that anyone could survive in that weather. I must have fallen asleep because I woke up to see that I was still breathing. By the next day, I was ready to leave.

After leaving Starkville, we traveled south to Collins, Mississippi, to meet up with my cousin Anna Fae and her family, who welcomed us. They showed us around the area, took us over to Laurel, Mississippi, a place that a friend of mine from town was from. I enjoyed walking outside, looking around the area that my dad may have been at one time.

After two days, we left Collins and headed down toward Hattiesburg where I met another cousin. They were friendly, but not quite as friendly as Anna Fae's family had been. This was Anna Fae's sister. I couldn't put my finger on it, but something wasn't quite right. We all sat out on the front porch after we had been introduced to her family and talked about nothing in particular, just everyday things. We shared what it was like in California and invited them to come out. After about an hour or so, we all pitched in and ordered a bucket of chicken from a fast-food restaurant and talked some more. In our conversation, I soon found out why my cousin was a little standoffish. She began to tell me about when her mom and my dad were young. She told of how their mother had died and their father had married another woman, that their stepmother was very mean. She said that my father had left home and went to Saint Louis in his teens and left their mother there with her other siblings. She went on to say that her mother had married a man who drank and was mean to her. She had married to get away from her father and stepmother. As she went on with her story, it became clear that she blamed my dad for leaving her mother and younger siblings there. My dad had two older brothers that had left home before he did, but she was still holding a grudge against my dad. Now I understood why she wasn't as welcoming as her sister Anna Fae. She was still living in unforgiveness. It had been almost fifty years since my dad had left Mississippi, and she was still holding on to it. I could see the bitterness and hear it in her voice as she talked.

My mother had lived in McComb, Mississippi, which was west of Hattiesburg, but I didn't get the chance to visit it on this trip. We only had a certain number of days before we had to return to work.

My mother had also lived in Biloxi, so it was like a two-for-one to visit Biloxi too. After we had finished eating, we decided it was time to go. It wasn't like we were eating and running from a meal that we had been invited to; my husband and I had paid for most of the food. As we drove farther south toward the gulf of Mississippi, Lou and I talked about how she was still holding on to something that had happened almost fifty years earlier. It had not been my dad's fault that her mother chose to marry someone that would not make a good husband, but yet she blamed him for it. It is human nature to look for someone to blame, man or God. Looking for your past can sometimes be dangerous. Thank God that it wasn't anything that could harm us, but you never know what you will learn.

We came to Biloxi, Mississippi, where another of our cousins on my father's side lived with her family. I don't remember her name, but she was a beautiful spirited woman. She had cancer in her body, but she was one of the dearest people to meet. We felt very welcomed in her home. She took us down to the ocean and showed us around Biloxi. She showed us an abandoned hotel on the ocean that had been hit by a hurricane the year before. It was strange walking the street and in the park next to the ocean in Biloxi, imagining that my mother may have walked by this very way when she lived here. I wondered if she could see me in heaven and was she saying, "Yes, I was there, daughter." I loved my mother, but I know that it was better for her to leave this world in her suffering. To some people, it is enough to just have something that a parent or loved one left behind to hold and cherish, but I wanted to see where she had been in her travels in life. I imagined that I could feel her presence in the warm sunlight and in the gentle wind that touched my face. I knew that she had also married my brother's dad to get away from her home and moved to Biloxi with him, and that he had not been a very nice man either.

It is easy to have an idea of what someone went through, but to know exactly how it felt to them, you will never know. My cousin on my mother's side grew up in the same town as I did, wrote a wonderful book on her life. I'm not sure who started theirs first, and neither does it matter. I was still writing my story well after she was published, but our stories were as different as the east is from the west. This part of my journey didn't give me any kind of insight into my life today.

CHAPTER 2

I thought that if I went back to the beginning of my journey in life, maybe this would tell me something about what I was looking for. First of all, I started as far back as I could remember. My first memory was living in a house on a hill on Peach Tree Street in Red Bluff, California. I don't know why I remember it at the age that I was, but I remember it being white with red steps and red caps on both sides of the steps. It must have been a little after my sister Patsy was born. I remember standing in the kitchen looking up on a counter that loomed above my little two-year-old self. We had a yellowish-cream-colored radio on the counter that Mama would listen to while she was in the kitchen cooking dinner for my dad, Johnny Smith, from whom I was named (Johnnie Marie) after my dad.

Mama would whistle the tune of the song on the radio or hum along with it. She would sometimes sing along as well. I loved to hear her whistling. I would try to get my lips to make the sounds but couldn't master it, even now I can barely whistle for my dogs to come when I call them. Before Mama met my dad, she had been married to my brother's father, Robert Earl. She had evidently married the first man that asked her so that she could get away from home. I think that there is still a lot of that going on today. My mom and her husband had lived in Biloxi, Mississippi, and Shreveport, Louisiana. I would hear stories of how she was treated differently from her siblings while she lived at home. She would tell her friend how he loved to go to clubs to gamble and drink; he would get into fights. Mama told how he would break the blades off knives that other people had drawn on him. I am sure that is why she eventually left him and moved from the South out to California. Some of her family had already left and moved to California before her. While living with Robert Earl, she had three miscarriages in her seven years of marriage to him before she had a child to live at age twenty-five. Five years later, she had me, Johnnie Marie, when she met my dad. "I suppose, Tee, that you would have called her Grandma May." Her name was May-Lee, but she went by May-Lee.

You would have loved her. She had light brown eye which is where you and I got our eye color from. Her smile was radiant with straight white teeth. She was a joy to be around when she wasn't in a lot of pain.

After Mama moved to Red Bluff, she met my dad, Johnny, who had recently been divorced from his first wife. They moved in together in the house on Peach Tree Street. Actually, she moved in with him; he owned the house. I suppose my dad didn't want to get married again right away because he had just gotten out of one marriage, and he was not a young man. Although he wanted children, he was not willing to marry my mother. Eventually, she had two children, Patsy and me, with him before she left him. My dad was the kind of person that could make you feel like you were nothing if you let him. I suppose it was his way of controlling you. If my mother hadn't left him when she did, she would have probably ended up weak and would not have lived as long as she did. They had begun getting into arguments. Mama was not going to let anyone else run over her. I suppose that I got some of my fight to survive from her. I remember Mama telling me that my brother, Buddy, would. take me for a ride in his little red wagon when I was around three years old. Buddy was his nickname. His name was Robert Earl, named after his dad the same as I was named after my dad. She told her friend that when she was married to my brother's dad, she would put dolls in the bed to pretend that they were her children. She said that when her husband came home from drinking and carousing in clubs, he would throw them out of the bed. From what I gathered while eavesdropping on some of their conversations, he was a very mean man when he drank.

My brother had been asking her for a little sister. She said that he really wanted one badly until he heard the little boy's sister next door telling on him. Mama said that he told her he had changed his mind about having a sister, but we know that it was too late because here I am, with outstretched arms and smiling. My brother loved me nevertheless. Mama said that he saved my life one day when he had taken me out to play. As far as I understood, Buddy was playing with me outside in the front yard when I must have wandered into the street. The house had two-foot-high bushes in front but no fence or gate. I suppose that the car didn't see me coming out of the yard. Buddy ran and saved me from getting hit, which I don't remember.

Anyway, my brother saved my life, and he loved me. My next memories are when we moved to Elm Avenue next to Annie May's Cafe. Mama had left my dad and moved out because they were getting into physical altercations. I overheard mama telling her friend Susan Hamilton that she slung my dad over behind the heater—it was one of those old-fashioned ones that sat out from the wall with the stovepipe that goes up into the upper wall or ceiling.

Susan Hamilton was the only adult that we didn't have to say Mrs. or Mr. to, but we had to say her whole name (Susan Hamilton).

Patsy was a toddler at this house; I have a picture of her on her birthday with a cake that had only one candle on it. It's the only baby picture we have of any of us girls as babies. We had a little black-and-white dog named Spotty that we loved very much. Mama used to let us let him into the house to play with. Once, our cousins Jackie and Janice came to visit us from out of state with their dad. They were afraid of Spotty, so we couldn't let him in when they were there. I was mad and wanted them to leave so that our dog could come into the house to play with us again. This is where my life began to change from the normal family life to a downhill roll. Mama said that when my dad didn't come to visit me often enough, I would get sick until he came by.

I also remember Buddy taking me trick-or-treating on Elm Avenue. Down the street about four or five houses on the other side of Annie May's café, there was a big two-story apartment that I was afraid to pass by. With my childlike imagination, I thought that I saw a pumpkin head fall off of someone standing at the top of the stairs and roll down the steps that night. I never liked passing by that house after that. I don't remember much about our house on Elm Avenue, but I do remember that I was happy playing with my first puppy—Spot—my baby sister, and my brother here. I don't know what happened to Spot when we moved.

A couple of years later, Mama met and married my baby sister Patsy's dad, Charlie Morgan. We moved into his house on Dennis Street. He kept chickens in the backyard. I hated living there. Sometimes I had to feed them or go look for eggs; I was in the fourth year of my life now. Sometimes the chickens would peck me. There was chicken poop everywhere you walked in the backyard, even on the grass. I remember trying to walk between the black and white drops of poop. I didn't like Rita's dad either. I didn't know why, but there was something about him that I just didn't like. Sometimes, I wonder if that is where my brother picked up that foul evil spirit, because after we left his house is when my brother started acting different toward me. I can't say that he molested him because I don't know for sure, but he had molested someone's child a few years later. Mama only stayed with Mr. Charlie for a couple of months.

She moved from his house when she was still pregnant with my baby sister, so something had to have gone very wrong. I never found out what it was. When Mama left Mr. Charlie (that is what we always called him), we moved to Orange Street, across the street from the

Wine-o Barrel behind Robinson's store. The store was on Brook Stone, the same street that cousin Adell and cousin Naomi's mom, Aunt Mary-Lee, lived on.

The Wine-o Barrel was a place behind the store in an open lot that had a big trash barrel. I suppose there were similar places in other cities. Some of the out-of-work and retired men would congregate in a huddle, shooting the breeze about the latest news and passing around a bottle of wine that one of them had scraped up enough money to buy. When the weather would turn cold, someone would light a fire in the barrel so that they could keep warm. When darkness fell, they all dispersed and went to their own homes or places of shelter.

Our house was painted an aqua blue color; I guess I remember that because being an artist, colors always interested me even whenI was very young. I take after my Father God. I love to take a bunch of plain colors or flowers that by themselves are just plain or drab and make something beautiful out of them. I was so happy to move to that house on Orange Street out of Mr. Charlie's house. We were living there when Rita was born.

There was a crippled lady who lived on the corner next door. Her house faced Douglas Street; we lived behind her, facing Orange Street. She grew roses all around her yard inside of a tall white fence. There was a gate that led from our house through the backyard of hers. Once in a while Mama would send me over to her house to borrow something, like sugar or milk.

After Mama had Rita is when I first remember that Mama began to get sick. I used to have to change Rita's dippers, give her a bath, and give her a bottle—a lot for Mama. I had to learn how to stick the safety pin into the diaper without sticking Rita. I remember sticking myself in the fingers a lot trying to not stick her. We didn't have disposable diapers in those days with the sticky tape closures; only the cloth diapers that I had to wash out to be used over and over again. I had only just turned five years old the month before Rita was born, but somehow I knew that I had to be more responsible for my sisters. Sometimes I was having fun playing outside and I would have to come into the house and take care of Rita. After a while, I began to understand that it was my responsibility to take care of my sisters and not play as much. I don't remember being a child much after that. Of course I know that I wasn't an adult yet, but instead of thinking about playing as much, I would began to be concerned about things like if we had food in the house to cook, check to see if Rita needed to be changed. Things that I shouldn't have had to worry about I was worried about.

I think that Mama got some kind of welfare aid for my brother that helped pay the rent. Mama also got a little child support from my dad for Patsy and myself. It was very little at that time; my dad only had to pay her twenty dollars a month for two children. It couldn't have gone very far. I do remember that Mama couldn't work much, so we had to move to Douglas Street because she couldn't pay the rent one too many times at the house on Orange Street. As a result, we packed up for another move.

Our next house was about a half block from that of the lady's that we had been renting from but on the other side of the street on Douglas Street. I remember that we walked back and forth from one house to the other, carrying things in our arms when we moved. It was at this house that whatever childhood I had left fled from my life. I just tried not to think of the bad things that happened to me sometimes. I used to pretend that I was a fairy like Tinker Bell. Fairies could hide, and no one could find them because they were so little. They could see you, but you couldn't see them. I would have given anything to be one at that time.

It was also at this house that I found out that I was black. It was almost like being born with a curse on your life to me at that time in my life. I didn't know that Adam who is called the 1st Adam had passed down a curse to all of man kind from his disobedience to God in the garden in Genesis 3:17. Jesus the Christ the 2nd Adam bore the curse for all of man kind on the cross. When we trust in Jesus' finished work on the cross and receive Him as our Savior we are freed from the curse. John 8:24 and Galatians 3:13. I never thought about being black or white. One Christmas, Mama bought me this little rubber doll that had molded black hair, black eyes, and brown skin. I told Mama that I didn't want that burnt-up doll. When she told me that it was the same color that I was, I was shocked. The only black people that I had seen on TV at that time almost were Amos and Andy, and they made me feel ashamed to be black the way that they portrayed colored people.

The next time I saw a white person when my brother was around, I wanted to know what they were if I was supposed to be colored. He said that they were "white patties." He taught me how to sing a song. He said, "If any one calls you the n-word, you say, 'White patty, white patty, you don't shine, I'm a little colored girl, kiss my behind.'" I waited about four years, waiting for somebody to call me the n-word. I suppose that in a small poor town where all of the children play together, you don't think about color or race because you are all trying to survive. But now I had a new dilemma. I didn't know what a nigger was either—go figure—and I still didn't think that I was colored. At school, we all played together at recess and had no problems. Unfortunately, racism is learned and passed down to innocent children to carry on from generation to generation. There are good people and bad people in every race. I love fellowshipping with my white, Hispanic, and brothers and sisters in other races. We all have something to give and share. I have heard it said that black people clap on the first beat and the white ones clap on the second and everyone else in between so that no praise will be left out for God. My mother never told us that white people were bad. I believe that she had equal white friends as she did black friends, one of each. My brother had learned the song from one of his friends at school. If Mama knew that he had taught me about the n-word or to sing a song about a white patty, she would have made me go get a switch and tore up my legs with it. I never heard Mama talking bad about any race except the one time that my brother's principal paddled his behind. She told him that she would be the one to get his behind and no redneck had better ever touch him. Yet another dilemma: now just what was a redneck?

I started kindergarten at the house on Douglas Street. My first day of school, I got into a fight with five other girls at one time. I had been called Marie at home, my second name, ever since I was little. My mother registered me in school by my first name, Johnnie. I was named after my dad because he wanted a boy and didn't get one. I didn't like school from the very first day. My brother, being five years older than I was, taught me how to do cursive writing and some reading, so when the teacher wanted to see if we could write our names, I didn't print it; I wrote mine in cursive, Marie. My teacher, Mrs. Ball, told me that I couldn't write like that, and she said that I had to write my first name, Johnnie.

The teacher called me Johnnie at roll call the first day of school. The kids at school teased me when they heard it and called me Johnnie. They said that I had a boy's name. On the way home, they started to tease me again, and we got into a fight. I won. A few of us became good friends after that; later we all became friends. There wasn't anyone else for us to play with. At school when we started to learn how to print, it was harder for me because I was already writing and had skipped over printing, and I would forget and try to write words. I liked the little squiggly tails on the cursive words; printing was too plain.

The new house that we moved into on Douglas Street had two bedrooms in it. Mama slept on the couch in the living room most of the time. Sometimes she slept on one of the bottom bunks of the two sets that were in the girls' bedroom on either side of the room. The girls' room was in the front of the house. When she felt well enough to get up from the couch, she would sleep in our room. The other bedroom was in the back of the house. That was where my brother slept. We had to go through a corner of his room to go to the bathroom.

One day when Mama was sick up in the front of the house and my sisters were asleep, I had to go to the bathroom. My brother was in his bedroom, lying on his bed. He called me over to his bed and told me to lie down by him, which I obediently did, thinking that he was going to teach me something. He was always showing me how to read or make something. He told me to pull my panties off, and he got on top of me. He said he was doing this to show me that he loved me. It hurt me, but because my brother had always taken care of me and loved me, I didn't think that he was trying to hurt me, so I let him. After that, I was afraid to go to the bathroom, and I would hold my pee as long as I could unless I knew that he wasn't in his room. I would hurry in and out as fast as I could. Once in a while he caught me when I came out of the bathroom and told me to come get in his bed. I hated this game, but I didn't know what to do because Mama was sick.

I never told my dad because he didn't live with us, and I didn't see him often. I loved him so much, why didn't he want to be with us? Yes, he would come visit us sometimes, but not often. Mama said that once I had gotten pneumonia and nothing that the doctor did would help until my dad came to see me. When we were a few years older, he started picking us up to go to the Seventh Day Adventist church with him. He would come by and pick us up some Saturday mornings and take me and Patsy to church with him. I don't think that it lasted too long because I don't remember him coming to pick us up much until we moved to the next house. Besides, he didn't take Rita with us, and I didn't like to leave her.

It was during this time that I begin peeing on myself at night, not because I was a sleep but because I did not dare go to the bathroom at night. Mama was sick most of the time, and I didn't want to tell her what Buddy was doing to me. Mama went to the hospital and had surgery to remove some tumors that were making her sick. While she was in the hospital, we stayed with our aunt Mary Lee. That was little better, but I missed Mama so much. Sometimes our cousins would take out cardboard games to play; that was fun. We didn't have any board games. I wasn't used to playing with my cousins, so I stayed in the house most of the time.

After Mama came home and was feeling better, Buddy didn't mess with me, so I didn't say anything. When I look back, I guess he thought he would get caught when she was feeling well enough to move around the house. Sometimes there was so much stress in my life I needed to get away from this real world that I lived in, so I would get into the closet and put clothes or a blanket over my body and hide in the bottom of the closet on the floor for a while. There were times that someone looked into the closet looking for me but didn't know that I was there. Sometimes I would fall asleep under the clothes. Once I tried to run away, but I didn't know where to go, so I went and hid under the porch. I was afraid of the spiders and bugs, but it wasn't as bad as my life was. After what felt like a few hours, I came out. I joined the book club to get fiction books to read and escape for my life.

One day, Mama was washing the clothes and saw some blood in my underwear. I was so glad that she would finally find out what Buddy was doing to me and make him stop. She took me to the doctor. The doctor put a tub in my private place and took some tests that hurt me just as bad as Buddy had. After the doctor examined me, he told my mother that I was just starting my menstrual cycle early. How stupid can a doctor be? Starting a menstrual cycle at five or six years old? Now I was afraid to go to the doctor again because he would hurt me down there too. I didn't know what to do. I was afraid of my brother and started to dislike him. We began to be enemies after that.

By the time that I was seven, Mama was getting sick again. I was doing most of the washing for our family, so I guess my mother never thought about checking my underwear anymore. By the time that I was eight, I was doing most of the cooking too. Buddy cooked once in a while. Most of the time he was gone with his friends, and I was glad. There was no way I could go back to being a child. In all ways, I was the woman of the house at eight years old. I was doing everything that a mother would be doing. I was raising the kids, cooking, and washing for the family and having sex with the man of the house—my brother. Even though my life was turned upside down, I know now that God was with me even then, although I didn't understand then.

Sometimes during this period of my life, I would have dreams about being in a doorway, and someone was trying to pull me through the door. Somehow I knew that if I went through that door, it would be bad for me. On the other side, someone else was trying to stop them and pull me back to the safe side. I would lie there awake sometimes just thinking about how things was and say the prayer that Mama had taught us: "Now I lay me down to sleep, I pray the Lord my soul to keep. If I should die before I wake, I pray the Lord my soul to take." Even as I sit here and write these pages, I am crying. They say that it is healing to get your feelings out.

When I lived on Douglas Street, there was a lot more that I remembered, probably because now I am getting older. Once Daddy came and took Patsy and me on a train trip to visit some of his family in St. Louis. I wanted Rita to come with us, but she wasn't his daughter, and he didn't take her. I remember that trip was one of the best two weeks of my young life, because I didn't have to worry about anything. I could just be a child and have fun. Patsy and I played up and down the train jumping from one train car to the other over the connections. Daddy had got sleeping accommodations for us to sleep on the train. We played and talked after he sent us to bed until we fell asleep. When we were in St. Louis, I only had to look out for myself and no one else, not even Patsy. We met a cousin named Billy, and he taught us how to catch fireflies. We stayed outside playing until after they turned the streetlights off.

When we returned to Red Bluff from the train trip, things went back to the way they were pretty much. My brother didn't bother me though. I thought it was probably because I was getting older and he thought that I would eventually tell Mama.

For Easter, Daddy would come over and take us shopping for an Easter dress and shoes. Daddy would just take Patsy and me with him and leave Rita; I would ask if she could come with us, but most always, the answer was no. I remember that once Daddy took Rita with us and bought her a dress; she was so happy. It was understood that her dad should do that for her and she couldn't come with us. I didn't like that. I knew that it would hurt her. I was sensitive to her needs; she was like my little girl. I wanted her to have nice things too. Daddy would take us to Sears and Roebucks and buy us these beautiful rayon or nylon dresses (I don't remember which) in pastel colors and shiny patent leather shoes that other children would envy. I hated mine. It just brought more attention to me. I was made to be aware of my weight early in my life. I enjoyed cooking for the family because I could taste the food while I cooked it. Eating seemed to be the only thing that gave me peace, and cooking gave me satisfaction if everyone liked it. I didn't think about us not having much food, that anyone would care how it tasted, as long as we ate.

Daddy would make sure that everybody in the store knew that I was fat. When I look at some of my old childhood pictures though, I really wasn't as fat as I was made out to be; but in my head, I believed that I was huge. I was a little husky for the time that we lived in. I don't really know how I even got a little overweight, with food being in such a small supply, except that the food we had wasn't very healthy—a lot of rice and bread sandwiches. We had sandwich spread, sandwiches with white bread and also sandwiches with sugar and a little butter on it a lot, with a glass of sugar water, and once in a while cornbread crumbled up in milk. Having bologna on bread was a delicacy.

When my dad took us to the department store, he would tell the clerk in a loud voice for everyone in the store to hear him to take me to the big ones. He'd say, "Take her to the big 'uns." I wanted to hide behind the clothes racks or run away or just disappear, but I just held my head down, refusing to cry and walked to the chubby section behind him and the clerk with Patsy tagging along. I am so glad that God loves me for me. He is the perfect example of a true father. I thank God that I discovered in his word that we are beautifully and wonderfully made. My heavenly Father loved me from the foundation of the world and knew me before I was formed in my mother's womb. My hope is in Christ and nothing less, in Jesus's love and righteousness.

On Easter Day, we would dress up in our finery and walk to the south part of downtown Red Bluff to the Easter egg hunt that the city put on every year for the whole town. Everyone was looking for that prized egg. There were hundreds of kids it seemed—the girls in their Easter dress and ruffled folded-down socks, the boys in their little sweater suits. Other children in plain everyday wear, searching through knee-high grass that the city let grow for this special event. The hunt took place in front of the train station that was just at the edge of town. I couldn't even tell you what the prize was now. Although we never found the treasured golden egg, we would go home with a half dozen or so each of brightly colored boiled eggs to eat for the next few days. Sometimes I think Mama sent us just so we could have something to eat.

While on Douglas Street, one of our aunts, Aunt Jenny, moved in the house behind us. There was an alley between the back of the houses. The alley had grown weeds and grass except on the path that went from our house to theirs. Their house faced Elm, the street behind us. Sometimes Mama would go over and visit Aunt Jenny and take us with her to play with our cousins when she felt good enough. We would pick the blackberries in the backyard that grew next to the alley in the summer, and Mama and Aunt Jenny would can them or make a pie.

Later when Aunt Jenny moved out, Susan Hamilton moved into the same house. Mama and Susan Hamilton where really good friends. I remember Mama laughing at times in this house after she had gone to the hospital and had her first surgery to remove a tumor. Sometimes she would sing when she cooked in the kitchen. She would sing or whistle, "Swing low, sweet chariot, coming for to carry me home." When she would get to the part about, "I looked over yonder and what did I see, coming for to carry me home, a band of angels coming after me, coming for to carry me home." I would sometimes look to see if they were coming. Now I wonder if she wanted them to come for her then, if she was still in pain and because of the hard life she had, trying to feed and take care of us—if she wanted God to take her home.

Once when the Fourth of July came, she was feeling up to it and had a little money from doing housework, Mama took us to the park in Chico on a picnic, the park in Red Bluff was by a swift river, and she didn't think it was safe. The park in Chico had a waterway running into it from a smaller creek that had been dammed up to create a large swimming area. I loved to go to Chico. Mama used to collect S&H Green Stamps from the store. When you bought something, they would give you stamps based on the amount of things you bought. I would get to dampen the stamps with a moist face towel and put them into the book. I had to be real careful and put them in straight. When the book got full, you could go to the S&H trading store and trade them in for things. Mama would save them until she got a lot of books filled and take them to Chico to trade them in for blankets, an iron, and other things that we needed. We girls loved to watch the *Captain Sacto* show that aired out of Chico on our black-and-white TV. Once they had a contest to be on the show. I put in for it and got the chance to go on the show. Mama had to drive us to Chico to be on the show. Thankfully, she had stamps to trade at the time. It would have been unthinkable to use gas just to go to the show. When I went to school, I told the kids that I had been on TV and was now a movie star. The kids thought that I was lying about being on the show, but I knew the truth. I figured they were just jealous.

Although Mama didn't have much money, when a need arose, she seemed to find a way to provide for us the best way that she could. Once Mama bought a goat because the doctor said that Rita needed to have goat milk to drink. Rita was kind of sickly when she was little. The doctor said she had a bad heart. Her lips would turn blue when she got cold. I was responsible for taking care of her most of the time and looking out for Patsy too. Whenever Rita got hurt, I would get into trouble for not watching her better. Once she cut her foot on some glass in the backyard, and I was the one that got my behind whipped. Mama had this peach tree in the yard that never had good peaches on it; they always stayed like hard green little knots. We had to go get our own switch off it to get whipped with. I remember bringing back a little switch about a foot long and Mama made me go back and get a long one. Most of the time it was me getting the switch for myself for something to do with Rita.

One of my favorite memories in this house was the chinaberry tree and the green lawn in the front yard; such simple things could cause joy. I remember that there were these seeds on the chinaberry tree that when they dried, we threw them up into the air and they flew like a helicopter. They would go twirling around in the air. I also remember that in the lawn was a small hill and me and my sisters would roll down it laughing and screaming. We would itch like crazy afterward until we got a bath, but it was fun.

Once when Mama was in remission of the cancerous tumors that the doctors found in her later and she felt better, we had gone fishing with long cane fishing poles to catch for dinner. When I was growing up, it wasn't nearly as expensive to fish as it is now. We dug our own worms and didn't have to pay for fishing license. I think that Mama did need a license because she would tell one of us to come take the fishing pole if someone came up to where we were fishing. While we were out fishing, we kids would wonder around when we got bored and the fish were not biting.

Another time we went fishing, I found where someone had built a fire and had left before we got there. When the ashes of a fire get cold, they turn white, but you couldn't tell if they are really all the way out or if there are still hot embers underneath. I didn't see any smoke coming out from the fire, so I told Rita to put her foot on it to see if it was hot. I knew if they were hot, I would get my behind beaten. That was the only time that I didn't care that I got into trouble. I loved Rita, but I was tired of getting whipped because she got hurt; this time it was going to be worth it. Sure enough, the coals were still hot under the ashes and burned her foot. I got my behind whipped, but I didn't care; it was too tempting.

We would sometimes fish off the side of the road in a canal waterway or off a bridge. If a car came, we had to go down on the side of the bridge. This particular time, we were fishing in a channel that was connected to the river. Something bit my hook and jerked my fishing pole out of my hand. You could see the pole going down the channel as far as you could see until it turned out of sight. Mama said that it was probably a sturgeon fish that had somehow gotten upstream. I still enjoy fishing today. But I don't think that I ever want to catch anything that big or have it catch me.

One time Mama bought a pig and had a pen built for it in the backyard. I couldn't tell you where she got the money to buy it. We had to go feed it, which I hated. I thought that it might get out of the pen and get me. When the pig got big enough, she had my Uncle JR come over and kill it and help to butcher it. Mama also went to a chicken farm to get eggs to eat every now and then. Once when we were there getting eggs, the car wouldn't start when we got ready to leave. You had to go up a gravel hill road from the main road to get to the chicken farm, so we had to push the car until it started back down the hill.

Everyone was pushing from the sides of the car's back fenders, but I thought that if I turned around backward and sat on the bumper and dug in with my feet, it would give me more power to push the car. I am a thinker, but sometimes I underanalyze things, what can I say? So I sat on the back fender and dug in. It did help, but when the car started to go down the hill, I couldn't get off. I held on with my fingertips, trying not to fall off. I know that if I did, I would get scarred up bad, falling on the gravel road or get killed because the car was moving so fast down the hill. I know that it was God that sent an angel to help me stay on that car bumper.

Now I wonder what kind of crazy things my kids have done that I am not aware of since we left Red Bluff and moved to Sacramento. Every now and again, they will let something slip out what they have done when they were kids, like hiding and throwing watermelon rinds at cars when they passed by the street or walking over to the river by themselves that was about a half mile from our house. Another time after Mama passed away, we went to live with my dad in Red Bluff. We were on our way to do laundry at the Laundromat downtown. I fell out of the back of his truck while leaning over the side. When he turned a corner, I jumped up and ran to catch up with the truck and got back in before he ever knew I had fallen out. Thankfully, everyone drove fairly slow downtown in Red bluff anyway. I had scrapped my knees, but I hid them and the pain until we got back home.

Once Mama bought three little baby chicks. Mama and my brother Buddy built a chicken pen for them. There was one for each of us girls. We named our biddies and played with them and fed them. When they got big, one of them disappeared, so we shared the other two between us. About a month later, another one disappeared. When that happened, I had caught on that mama was killing our chickens and we were eating them. It was all right for me to eat the chicken after I found out what it was, but for some reason, I felt that the last one belonged to me. The next time we had chicken, I couldn't eat it.

I knew that Mama was cooking our chickens, and there was no way I could eat my own pet.

Buddy had turned on me now; he had started being mean to me. When Mama bought chickens home from the chicken farm, she would let him kill them. He would wring their neck and throw the chicken at me and laugh while I was running from the chicken that was flopping all around the yard. It seemed to me that every which way I ran, the chicken would flop that way too. Sometimes Buddy would be out playing football with his friends and would get musty under his armpits, and he would catch me if I walked by and put my head under his stinking armpits. He thought that it was funny. I had to go wash my face and neck because I could smell his funk going up my nose.

I really don't know how we survived. Most of our friends had dads in the home, but we didn't. Work was hard to find for the black men in town. They would go to the neighboring towns to get work. My dad worked at the lumberyard and would pay Mama a little child support for Patsy and me. Sometimes when she could, Mama would find a cleaning job with a wealthy white family on the outskirts of town. She would take us with her, and we had to play outside or stay in the car for a few hours while she worked. Once she had me come in and help her dust the tables in the house because she wasn't feeling well. She told me to make sure that I put everything back exactly the way it had been before I started dusting.

I remember that she had this white friend that lived on Washington Street just before it went down a steep hill. We would go to her house and pick figs off of a gigantic fig tree. I would be itching so bad that I couldn't wait to go home and take a bath to get some relief. The woman was the biggest woman that I had ever seen in my life. I think she must have weighed over four hundred pounds. In those days, you didn't see people that obese, as you do now. I think that she might have weighed maybe even five hundred pounds. She could hardly walk and when she sat in a love seat, she took up all of the room on it. I always wondered how she wiped herself, but I didn't smell her stinking. One day, I heard Mama telling a friend that her husband had to help clean her. She would give Mama vegetables— okra, corn, and tomatoes—that mama would can so that we would have food in the wintertime. Sometimes mama would make fish head stew with the heads of the carp and catfish that we caught. It tasted good, but I hated looking at it because the fish eyes were in it. In the summer, we would go and glean peaches from a peach field, and Mama would can those. That was the only time that I was glad when we went to a field because I was allergic to the peach fur and Mama didn't make me pick them. After we got them home and they were peeled, I did have to help cut them up though and help with the canning. That was all right because I could eat a piece every now and then when I was cutting them up. We also went and pick prunes in the fields to make extra money to live on by. Most of the families we knew went to the fields too. When we went to the prune fields, we would end up with diarrhea because we ate too many prunes when we were picking them. We also picked blackberries and wild greens on the side of the road when we went fishing; we had to watch out for snakes.

When Mama cooked the wild greens, she made steamed hot water corn bread to go with it. She would drop balls of seasoned cornmeal mixed with hot water on top of the greens while they were cooking and let it steam. Sometimes she would have me make corn bread in the oven if we had all the ingredients, or she would have me make it. I was scared to light the oven though. We used to have to twist paper and light it on a match or an eye on top of the stove and stick it to the pilot light under the broiler of the oven. Once I left the gas on too long and singed off my eyebrows, front edges of my hair, and the hair on my arm.

I would mash up the corn bread with the green juice and feed it to Rita or work the fish in my mouth to make sure that there weren't any bones in it before I gave it to her to eat. Rita was more like my child and I was her mama. I guess that's why my children were healthy. I had learned how to feed them with practice on Rita. My children didn't eat a lot of candy or sweets until they were older because we didn't have a lot of candy as kids. I wish that I knew more about how to raise them hugging and kissing them, but God knows that I did the best that I knew how. I pray for them, and trust Him to do the rest, and they are becoming great men and a beautiful young woman in heart and spirit.

My daughter's husband's family is a family of huggers. I am glad that she has that experience with them. I had never been a hugger until the recent years, and sometimes if I don't keep it purposed in my mind to hug my children when I see them, I convert back to the person that I learned so many years ago to be—fearful of being touched, never knowing if someone has an ulterior motive when they hug me, or if they are going to whisper something perverse and ugly into my ear. It wasn't just my brother that molested me. That is what this book is about. When men use you as trash, you don't have to stay on the ground. You don't just change overnight. It takes work; with God's help and strength, it becomes easier with time as you read the word of God often and learn how he desires to bless your life and your family. His promises are to you and your children's children. Just talk to the Father. Tell Him your heart. He is big enough to take it. You may have had a dad that wasn't a good example of love to you, but God the Father, Abba Father (daddy) is our example.

When you have lived a life of not being hugged or loved, or touched properly you forget to hug, and it is hard to touch or be touched. I must on purpose set myself to be the person that God called me to be. I let God know that I can't do it myself, that I need His help. When I say do it on purpose, it doesn't necessarily mean force yourself to do something—although sometimes it does require you to force it at first. I want to be a hugger, I desire to become a hugger; therefore I on purpose hug until it becomes a part of my life. Even just a small touch on the arm or hand on the shoulder can make such a big difference in lives. I want my children, grandchildren, and great-grandchildren to be whole and healthy, so I on purpose show them love now, instead of just loving them in my heart and never saying it with words or showing them with a loving and caring touch and hug.

Some of my older cousins say that they loved to come over to my mom's because she loved to have fun. My mother was a giving person. She loved people, and she loved laughing. The only problem with this is that I don't remember them coming over to visit my mom as much as they say they did, especially when she was sick. Maybe they came when I was a baby. In fact, I only remember them coming over a couple of time for her to babysit their children.

I heard Mama tell her friend Susan Hamilton that she was like the black sheep of the family. I do know that most of the time that she was sick. Hardly anyone came over to see her, except her friend Susan Hamilton. One of my uncles told me that he didn't know that my mom had cancer. He said that he thought that she just had a fat stomach. Even my own dad said that she was fat and lazy. If they only had just taken the time to see that she was really sick. But you have to forgive them. My cousins told me about how they used to go to my grandmother's and play and have fun; even Rita, now that she is an adult, remembers playing there once in a while. I remember a few times when we would go to Granny's to take pitchers as a group, with the rest of the family, for my grandmother's birthday. Most of the family pictures didn't even have Mama on them because she was always too sick to come, so she just sent us for the pictures. I don't remember my grandmother ever coming to see my mom when she was sick. She may have, but I don't remember it; and I think that I would have if she did.

CHAPTER 3

When I was nine or ten, we moved to Hickory Street. Mama was getting sicker and sicker at that time. Finally, she went back to the doctor, and they found out that she had more tumors in her stomach. When she went into the hospital for surgery, we went to stay with my grandmother Luella Osprey, this time until Mama got out of the hospital. My dad was so much older than my mom was when they got together that he didn't know how to take care of us. He was fifty-one years old when I was born, and I was the first of his offspring. I think his parents were dead already. I remember that Mama was suffering so much that she would put her hand on the TV, hoping to be healed when Oral Roberts, the TV minister, came on. I would see her praying that God would heal her.

There was really no decent food for her or us to eat that would help her body fight off diseases. Most of the time we ate cornflakes with water and tomato gravy (brown flour gravy with tomato sauce in it) with canned biscuits. For meat, my brother would go out with his BB gun and shoot robins to bring home for Mama to cook. Once Daddy brought us a squirrel, another time a pheasant; Mama cooked that for us to eat too. I know that some people here in the United States don't have even that to eat, and a squirrel would be a treat. I know that it was for us.

We were so malnourished that our hair had turned reddish in color. We looked like the African children with the extended bellies that you see on TV shows like what some of the TV ministers show on feed-the-children shows and others nowadays. We had sandwich spread, the kind with the pickle relish in it, on white bread for sandwiches and no meat. Our soda pop consisted of water with a little sugar in it when we could get sugar. Sometimes she would have a stick of butter, and we would make sugar and butter sandwiches, and it was a treat. Every now and again, Mama would get some money and send me to the store to get a pound of ground beef or pressed ham. My brother would make chili beans with the ground beef and canned kidney beans.

When we moved to Hickory Street, I finally got my chance to sing that song about the white patty. I was walking home from school and a little boy called me the n-word, so I gleefully sang in a singsong voice, "White patty, white patty, you don't shine. I'm a little colored girl, kiss my behind." I still had no idea what the n-word was supposed to be or why he was a white patty. I had heard of a hamburger patty. He just stood there looking at me and didn't know what to say, and neither did I, so I walked off with a smirk on my face. I think that is what gave me a sense of foolish pride that stuck with me for years to come. I felt that I was better than he was because I could sing that song and make him shut up. I think that was the only time that I got to use it though. There was no way that I was going to tell Mama what I had done. I knew that she would beat my behind. She was feeling better at the time I sang it.

I loved to read. When you read a book, you can be transported to anywhere you wanted to be. When I learned that I could check out books from the mobile library that came to the school once a week. I would check out as many books as the limit would allow me. You could be anybody and go anywhere when you are reading. It was at this house that I discovered why my brother had left me alone sexually. It had been a couple of years since he had bothered me, so I had put it in the back of my mind. I never felt comfortable around him because I never knew what mean thing he would try to do to me. He was not the loving brother that I once knew. One Fourth of July, he made some firecrackers out of bike spoke parts and threw one at me.

One day I went into the garage for something, and there he was with a neighbor's child. He had her standing on something, trying to do it to her. I told him that he had better never touch her again. I told him that if he ever messed with anyone else again that I would kill him, and I meant it. I believe that he knew that I would. I felt so bad because I thought that if I would have let him do it to me, he wouldn't have been trying to mess with anyone else. I carried that guilt for a long time. I hoped that I had stopped him in time. I was, after all, responsible for others wasn't I. No child should have that kind of weight on their shoulders, but I did. After that, I made sure that I never forgot what he did. I watched my sisters and their friends when they came over, I tried to be around them always. If one were missing for a short time, I would go look for them. I never caught him with any of them after that, but I had heard that he had been messing with another girl in town.

Although we were very poor, there where some fond and frightening memories in this house. First of all, it was one of the nicest houses that we had ever lived in. I have no idea how Mama could have afforded it. This house had this cute little fake well in the front yard with a large tree a few feet from it, good for climbing. It was the first house that had a garage even though we didn't put the car in it.

We rented it from the black people next door that owned their own business. Everybody knew the Man loves; they were the most influential black family in Red Bluff. I remember thinking that we were somebody because we lived next door to the richest black people in town.

Mama had turned in all of her S&H Green Stamp books that fall and bought beautiful Indian-print blankets for each of our beds. The house had one big bedroom that the girls slept in and a smaller bedroom for my brother. In the girls' bedroom, our beds were lined up across the room like three teepees in a row with a couple of feet between each one. I was so proud to look at those beds all made up. It was such a small thing, but it was special to me. It was kind of like a special on TV once about Oprah's school for girls in Africa. Those girls were so proud of their uniforms and white socks. Most of them had nothing at home, but when they were chosen to come to the school, they were so happy and proud you could feel it in your own chest just watching it.

It was on Hickory Street that Daddy decided to give Patsy and me piano lessons and bought us a used upright piano. Too bad he didn't decide to buy us food instead. I still don't understand why he didn't know that we needed food. When we went to his house on the weekends, we always had chicken or a beef roast. My dad didn't eat pork, so he didn't buy pork. We sometimes had vegetarian meat loaf, which was expensive as well. There was all ways plenty of food there. My dad worked for the High Sierra Pine Mill in Red bluff on Reading Road. He worked his way up from a laborer to the boiler room manager before he retired. It was a prestigious position for a black man at that time. My dad would tell us how that when he was in an early grade he had to quit school and go work in the field as did a lot of the black males in the time. He was very proud of the fact that he was able to teach himself to read.

On some occasion, he would take Patsy and me to work with him so that we could see what he did. He would let us push the button that would start or stop the machine that fed the giant logs through the shoots. They were cut into smaller that were used to cut and refine the giant logs that were fed through shoots. We were very proud of our dad when we were younger. He lived in an area of Red Bluff where not many black people lived in. Mostly, the black people that had money could afford to build a home in the river park area of Red bluff.

My dad signed us up with Mrs. Annie, and we started going to Annie May's cafe to take piano lessons. Mrs. Annie would give piano lessons in a room in the back of the store. None of our friends were taking them, so we didn't want to either; we wanted to be able to go play with our friends. After we had gone for a few months and learned to play a few songs on the piano, we started skipping our lessons to go play with our friends. Being kids, we had not thought our crime through. It never occurred to us that Mrs. Annie would ask Daddy why we were not coming to take piano lessons when he went to pay her.

When we got home from, taking piano lessons one day—or should I say from playing with our friends—Daddy was at our house. He asked us how our lessons were coming along and what song we had learned that day. I gave him the name of one of the songs that I had already learned. He told me to play it for him, and I went with confidence to the piano to play it. When I got through, he said that Mrs. Annie said that we had not come for a couple of weeks to take lessons. All that I could do was stare at him because I was busted. He pulled out a switch and pulled my dress over my head and beat my legs with the switch. That was the first and almost the last time that my dad ever punished me for doing anything wrong. Later, I didn't believe that he cared what I did because he never disciplined me for anything.

Daddy asked us if we wanted to keep taking piano lessons, and we said no. I really wished that he had made me take them now. Soon, the piano was out of tune and the lid broken, so we moved it out to the garage. A little kitten had found us, and Mama let us keep her. All three of us girls decided to name her after Mama; we called her Little May since our mother's name was May. Mama went back to using her married last name from when she was married to my brother's dad, Robert Earl. Little May used to get on the piano in the garage and walk across it when she wanted to come in the house. That was her signal to us to let her in.

A few months before we moved, my brother had caught a wild parakeet that had flown into our car window that we named Susie. She was very smart and was stronger than any tamed parakeet that we tried to mate her with. I don't know where we got the money to get another bird to try to mate with her. Maybe Mama thought that she could make some money if they had babies and she could sell them. If the male bird tried to mate with her, Susie would beat him up. Susie learned how to open the cage and let herself and the other bird out into the house. One day, she had gotten out and was under the dining table. I tried to shoo her out from under the table with my bare foot. She grabbed my big toe with her beak and wouldn't let it go. I was running and yelling around the house with her hanging onto my foot. By the time she did let go of my toe, she had pulled out a plug from it.

Occasionally, we would take her and the other parakeet outside in the shade so that they could hear the other birds and get fresh air. We would put a close pin on the cage so that Susie couldn't open it while they were outside. Eventually, she learned to get the pin off and open the cage door. After they made their escape back into the wild, it was the last that we saw of them.

Soon after we stopped taking piano lessons, Mama had to have surgery again. We kids had to go and stay with my grandmother while she was in the hospital. I used to hear her moaning and groaning all the time before she had the surgery. After Mama came home from the hospital, she started feeling better, but it didn't last. She started going to a little church down at the end of the block. I remember her and the people there praising the Lord. It mostly had white people in it. Sometimes I would see them do a dance. I remember watching them but I didn't know what it was about. I had never been to a church like it. After a couple of months, she quit going. I think it was because she was not feeling well. I believe that she did what is called backsliding because she started to dress up when she felt good enough and go out at night with someone. I believe that she was going out with a man to get money to buy food for us to eat because the next day she would have money to buy groceries with. Mama hadn't stayed in church long enough to be taught that God would provide for her needs and ours. When the food was gone at home, she turned to the worldly way of providing for us. I don't fault Mama because I knew that she loved us. I know because I love my children and will try to keep them safe by any means possible. Although I had started on that same path when my children were small, I have since learned to trust God for his provision. Mama was desperate to provide for her children, and she did it in the only way she knew how. I have learned that all the cattle on the hills belong to Father God, and because I am his child, I am his responsibility. This is something you can only learn when you decide to trust in God's word. You have to read his word to learn what his promises are and pray that he will give you the strength and faith to wait for him and to trust him. God's word said that he has given us all things pertaining to life and godliness to provide for us.

I remember Mama would dress up in this pretty black dress that had beautiful glass buttons down the front. My mama was beautiful when she dressed up. She had big beautiful light-brown eyes, straight white teeth, and her hair was down under her shoulders. She was only about five foot two or three inches with medium brown skin. She had dimples in her cheeks and a beautiful smile. After they took the tumors out of her stomach, it had gotten a lot smaller, she was beautiful. She told us that her hair used to be way down the middle of her back because of the Indian blood line in her mother's side. She would tell us how her mother would put it into two long braids when she went to school. She said that it got in the way and in her face when she was playing, so she would tie it under her chin to keep it from flopping around. She said that sometimes it got tangled and she couldn't get it loose, and she would get a beating about tying it under her neck.

One day we children were in the bedroom playing with the garage door opened to let a breeze into the house when Little May, our cat, came in with something in her mouth; she brought it in and put it in the closet, which had its door cracked open. We started hollering and yelling because we thought that she had killed a rat and brought it into the house. When she left it to go get the others, we looked and found out that it was a baby kitten. She had three in all—one for each of us. That was a special day. Later as the kittens grew, we couldn't get food for them, so we had to take them out to the county hospital and let them go. There were a lot of stray cats out there. They could get the scrap food they threw out from the patients.

I was always trying to think of something fun to do with my sisters. I made them a homemade Slip 'N Slide one summer. We had seen one on TV but knew better than to ask for one. I found some plastic somewhere and laid it out on the sidewalk. I ran water on it so that they could slide across it. Once, Mama showed me how to make homemade ice cream. It was a lot of work churning it with the rock salt and ice cubes, but it was fun eating it.

When I started school on Hickory Street, I went back to Clinton Elementary School where I had started to attend in kindergarten. I stayed at Clinton school until I got to the fifth grade. When I was in the fifth grade, they decided to integrate this school that was downtown; it was predominately white. We had to walk to Clinton school and then catch a bus to Olivehurst School. They only took one bus loaded with colored kids and a few Hispanics, but most of my friends were left there. It was not easy for me to make friends with the other kids because I was withdrawn and shy.

I hardly ever even played with my cousins, and meeting strangers was difficult for me. My cousins had started talking about boyfriends, the latest music out, and new clothes styles. I knew my clothes weren't as nice as theirs was. And because I was somewhat overweight, I didn't think a boy would want to by my boyfriend. I didn't have any friends at Sycamore School until a girl named DaNella moved to Red Bluff to live with her grandmother. Her parents had died and she and her brothers and sister had to move with their grandmother. She was light-skinned and wore her hair naturally kinky. All of us black girls in Red Bluff had our hair pressed. She wore secondhand clothes like we did. I think the reason that we became friends was because she was different like me.

DaNella's grandmother lived next door to where my dad lived in the river park, so when we went to my dad's, we could play with them. I didn't leave Rita at home anymore. DaNella had a little brother and sister named Marlene and Vincent that Rita and Patsy played with. If we went to visit my dad then Rita came with us, Mama would let her come with us, and Daddy didn't try to stop her anymore. I got a crush on DaNella's brother. He and my brother were friends, and he was about five years older than I was. I think that he knew that I liked him.

I am thankful that he must have been a decent person because he could have taken advantage of me too, but didn't. We had this big old oak tree that was next to their house. It had a swing tied on it. When I would sit in the swing watching him and talking with DaNella, he would sing to me. He did it to tease me, but I thought that I was in love with him. He never tried to touch me, and I'm glad because that would have ruined my fantasy. Just before school started again, Ms. Mitchell's house caught on fire. DaNella and her brothers and sister had to move out of town with Ms. Mitchell. I never heard from her again.

Mama would sign us up every year to get used Christmas presents and food boxes for needy families from the Salvation Army. The last year that we lived on Hickory, we got to go to a Christmas party out at a new center they had built. We had a nice dinner, and they gave us some new gifts along with the used bicycle for Rita. We had found a little tree about three and a half feet tall with no leaves on it to put the gifts under. My sisters and I made homemade ornaments to put on the tree out of colored paper. We strung popcorn and made a handmade star out of foil paper for the top. It is still the best Christmas that I can remember as a kid, and it was our last one together.

That last winter that we lived on Hickory, it snowed about three inches on the ground. I remember Mama telling us how to make snow milkshakes. She would tell us to make sure we only got the top snow that didn't touch the ground. It just so happened that we had sugar and vanilla flavoring when it snowed. We made snow balls and threw them at one another and made a two-foot snowman. That was another fun memory that I had at that house.

Moving to Cottonwood, California, this is the next to the last move before my mama died. Cottonwood is a little subdivision off to the north of Red Bluff; most all white people lived there. It was across the river from my world that I knew. We only lived there for the summer, so I pretended that it was our summer home. The house was small only one bedroom and a washroom, which Mama made part of it to be a bedroom for Buddy. There were no other houses for at least a block or two. The other houses had been torn down for the freeway to come through. The property was next to the place that they were constructing—Interstate 5 Freeway—and most likely going to be torn down also. It was a new highway coming through Red Bluff. It was an alternate from Highway 299. They had only dug out the dirt for the highway and had not begun to pave it yet when we moved there. My sisters and me used to take a cardboard box and slid down the steep incline after the highway workers left for the evening and on weekends.

We girls had a lot of fun there with each other because there was no one else to play with. I remember digging a little swimming pool for us there, which was more of a mudhole. We found a bag of cement that someone had left at the construction site of the freeway by the house. It was so hot in that dry dusty place that last summer before Mama passed away that I was trying to find a way for us to cool off. After I dug the hole, I tried to mix the cement up and put it around the sides of the hole. We didn't have enough cement so the water was dirty when we put water in the hole. We would scrape our legs on the lumpy cement, but it was still more than what we had. When we decided that we had enough scraped knees, we would hang a water sprinkler on a tree and run through it.

When school started, we moved back to Red Bluff, this time to Washington Street. I was eleven; we stayed at this house just about a year because it was in the beginning of the next summer that Mama died. I started school at Parsons Junior High School. It had a sixth grade and a seventh grade. It was the year that Martin Luther King Jr. was assassinated. Mama had started getting really sick. I was still doing most of the cooking and what little cleaning that I knew how to do. With Mama being so sick most of my life, I only knew how to do surface cleaning. My brother Buddy cooked once in a while when he was home, but I did all the washing and most of the cooking. There was a Sanctified Church across the street where we lived, and on Wednesday night in the summer, they would open the door and we could hear the music. Sometimes Mama would let us go over to the church. She never went back to church though. Sometimes when we didn't have any food, she would go out with this man. He would never come into our house, but I knew that she was going out with him. I know that she got money from him even though she never said it. When she came home, she would have money for me to go to the store to buy food. Once a few months before Mama passed, she sent me over to Mr. Charlie's, my sister Rita's dad's house to get some money that she had called and asked him for. She had gotten too sick to go out with her man friend by then.

When I went to get the money, he was looking at me funny when he handed it to me. He scared me; something just felt really bad to me, so I took the money and hurried out of the house. He used to keep it real dark in the house. When I got to the door, I ran and jumped off the porch. As I was coming down next to the porch, my leg hit a nail that was sticking way out. It cut a long gash on the side of my ankle, and as I was just about to land on the ground, it also cut another long gash out of the inside of my leg by my knee. I bled all the way home that was about nine blocks. Mama showed me how to clean it and put some Mercurochrome on it to keep it from getting infected. She wasn't able to take me to the doctor for stitches. Those are also scars that I carry around today.

Mama was a little superstitious. I guess she got it from growing up in the South. She used to tell us not to walk under a ladder or break a mirror. She would say, "Don't walk behind that black cat." I suppose that I had a little rebellion in me because I didn't believe that I would get bad luck doing these things. I would make it a point to walk under a ladder. I would even break mirrors on purpose, or if I saw a black cat, I would purposely go walk behind it. I don't know why; I just was determined that I would not have bad luck from superstitions in any case I couldn't see my life getting any worse. Whenever it thundered, when it rained, Mama would make us turn off the TV. She said that lightning would strike our house. I didn't think that part was superstition. I just thought that it would draw the electricity from the lightning.

I was growing up now, and sometimes I left Patsy and Rita at the house with Mama. I didn't believe that Buddy would bother her because of what I had told him, and she was getting older and would tell me if he tried. I think that was why he didn't like me anymore, but I didn't care. I would kill him if I found out the he was messing with one of my sisters and he knew it.

On Washington Street, I got my first boyfriend, sort of. I was embarrassed of him and didn't want anyone to know about us. His name was Charles, and he lived next door. He was crippled in one leg. I think that he had polio when he was younger, so he walked with a limp. He was kind of a nerd at school. Patsy and his sister Mary were friends, so we would go over to their house and play. In the summer, we would stay outside until it was dark because it was so hot in the house with the little window fan. One time, Charlie and I sneaked around the back of his house, and he kissed me. I didn't like it, and I kept spitting to get the feel of his tongue off my mouth. His lips were wet, and I didn't like his spit on my mouth. He tried to put his hand on one of my breast that I had just started to get, and I pushed him away and went back into the house. I didn't like people touching me. That was the end of that short courtship.

By the time school let out for the summer, Mama was so sick now that all she did was moan and pray, "Lord have mercy on me," and lie on the couch. God had mercy, He took her out of her misery and pain. When she got her monthly, I had to help her change her pads and undergarments. I think that was another reason that I tried to stay outside because of her moaning. It scared me, and I didn't know what to do for her. Even though some people look at me as being a strong woman, there were times in the past that I knew I was a coward. It is only the strength of God that keeps any of us from turning tail and running in hard situations, or stubborn foolish pride. It was only a few weeks later that she had to go into the hospital I suppose that our relatives felt that we could stay at home alone now. We only saw Mama alive once after that. I saw her in my nightmares for years after she died. I have learned to cast down evil imaginations and thoughts that try to exalt themselves above the knowledge of God now. I haven't had one in a several years now. During Mama's last days at home, one day, I had been cooking and was washing dishes when my brother came home and said something smart to me. We had already gotten into it earlier that week. On the Fourth of July, he had made more firecrackers and threw them at me. He also threw some fire at me with something and singed all the hair off one of my legs. Buddy had become very hateful toward me. He tried to hit me with his fist and knocked a hole in the wall in the hallway; he may have killed me or hurt me seriously by aiming at my head as he was. So later that day when he said something to me (I don't remember what he said, but I had had enough), I tried to stab him in the back with the fork that I had in my hand while washing dishes when he turned around to open the refrigerator. As I went to stab him, I slipped and fell from some water that I had gotten on the floor and stabbed myself in the wrist. I am thankful that I didn't stab him with it. I couldn't use my hand for a few weeks. Mama was too sick to even take me to the hospital; she just put some red medicine on my wrist and tied it up. My wrist was stiff for a couple of months. I still have one of the scars from the tines on my wrist even now. About a month before the end of summer, the hospital must have gotten a hold of Buddy and told him that Mama didn't have much time to live because he got us all into the car and took us out to the hospital. I don't even know if he had drivers licenses or not, but he took us out to the Shasta community hospital where she was. The nurses wouldn't let us kids in, so he sneaked us in to see her when they were not looking. That was the last thing I remember of kindness that he did for us. Mama had plastic tubs coming from her nose. Her eyes seemed much larger than the usual large light-brown beautiful eyes that she smiled at us with. They were sunk in dark. The cancer had eaten away a lot of her flesh and left her face looking hollow. I just stood there and cried. I didn't know what else to do. Buddy was seventeen, I was twelve, Patsy was ten, Rita was seven, and Mama was gone. I remember Daddy coming to pick us girls up from the house; he took Rita with us because her dad had moved to Oakland with his new wife. Buddy went to live with my grandmother until he turned eighteen. That summer was one of the worst summers of my life. I cried until I couldn't cry anymore. And when I thought that it couldn't get any worse, it did. Rita's dad and stepmother came and took her a few weeks later. I wanted to hide her. I wanted to protect her, but I was a child, only twelve. I went to my aunt and asked her to please help make them give her back. She said that she couldn't because they had legally adopted her. So I cried some more. It was like cutting my arm off. This was my child that I had raised that they were taking, and I couldn't do anything about it. I have to stop writing this for a while because it hurts too much to try to write it. I can barely see the computer, and my eyes are hurting from crying, and it is hard to breathe. I didn't think that it would hurt so much now, but I am not just remembering it, I am living it again.

CHAPTER

4

My dad's house was very nice; he built it when he remarried for the second time, not choosing to marry my mother. The two-bedroom house was one of the nicest houses that black folk owned in Red Bluff. It was in a part of town where the middle-class white lived and very few blacks. All the rooms were extra large; both bedrooms were big enough to make two bedrooms out of each one if you wanted. Our bedroom had a closet that went from one side of the room to the other. The house had a large sunroom that stayed nice and toasty in the winter with the sun shining in. It was a good place to go and read, but hot as heck in the summer. The house held only the bare minimum of furniture. The bedrooms held only a double bed and dresser in each, with two nightstands. My dad bought quality furniture but didn't believe in frills or extras. The living room had a custom-made sleeper couch, a platform rocking chair, and an old floor-model radio that I have in my home now. When Mama passed away, we were at least able to get the TV from our house, so it was also there. The TV played out after a few months; one of the tubs went out and my dad refused to pay money to get it fixed. The large eat in kitchen had a sturdy table sitting in the middle of the kitchen with four chairs sitting around it. And it had a large box freezer on one wall and a separate refrigerator; the whole house seemed empty and lonely. The house seemed to be crying out for love. With nothing to do to occupy myself, I started reading again to take my mind off my own life and grief of losing my mother. The books that I read were not the best to encourage a good life. I read *True Confessions* magazines, and others of that nature. My goal in life was to be a "kept woman." They seemed to have the best life, according to the magazines. They didn't have to worry about anything, or so I thought. That just goes to show how confused you can get when you don't understand Satan's devices. Satan will deceive us any way he can; this is what he used on me. Satan wanted to destroy my life ever since I was very young. As he wants to do to every human being because he hates God, and because we were made in God's image. He wants you to believe that no one loves you, especially not God. Because he knows that if we believe that God loves us, then we would believe his word and obey it. Satan knows that God planned to give us the best in life, not to take away from our lives. Living with my father proved to be not good at all; he was very strict and domineering. My sister Patsy and I had to be in the house by the time the sun went down. We had to go to bed at 9:00 p.m. in the summer or winter regardless if it were still light outside or not. Even when I was fifteen and Patsy was thirteen, our bedtime didn't change. We took to sneaking out at night and cutting school on weekdays. On Saturdays, Daddy would let us go to our cousins to visit after we would come back from the Seventh Day Adventist church that he attended. I say that he attended because as soon as we were released from the main sanctuary to go to our classes, we kept going out the door to the store or sit in my dad's truck until church was out. The problem with us only being able to visit our cousins is that we weren't that chummy with the girl cousins at that time. Sure we would talk with a couple of them at times, but the majority of the time, we got along better with the boy cousins. Patsy had had a fight with one of the female cousins after my mom passed because she said that she was glad our mother had died. Sometimes kids can be heartless and ignorant. I was very shy and withdrawn. I didn't know how to hold a conversation with girls at school or my girl cousins. I could never think of anything to say back to them when they asked me something to keep a conversation going. I would always give a one or two-word answer back that would not promote conversation, just yes or no. They liked to do drill team moves for school, and I always felt too fat to join in.

I had tried out for a cheerleader once and was too embarrassed and self-conscious to go back to see the results. I never knew if I had even been picked or not. The boy cousins made things and did fun things, like making motor bikes out of bicycles and motors from lawn mowers. They liked to go swimming in the summer and go bowling when we cut school; the girl cousins couldn't go swimming because their hair would get messed up. I had learned how to use a hot comb on my own hair and Patsy's hair when Mama couldn't do it, so it didn't bother us when we went swimming. We hooked up with the boy cousins and cut school, and yes, we even stole together. We would go into the stores like Montgomery Wards and JC Penney with an empty shopping bag that we blew up like a balloon for it to look full. When we came out, it still looked full, but it was full of clothes and personal needs now. We started stealing clothes because Daddy would buy us old-fashioned things to wear. Once when I asked him for a bra, he asked what it was. Then when I had to try to explain to him what I needed, he finally said, "Oh, you need a brassiere." I had never heard a bra being called a brassiere before. He embarrassed me so bad that I said that I would never ask him for anything again, especially any female items. We were coming into the age that we needed personal items. When we bought clothes home, he didn't really question us about where we got them. Once he did ask where we got something from, and we said that someone gave them to us; he never bothered checking to see if it was true. My dad was twenty years older than my mother. I suppose that by the time I became a young teen, he didn't have the energy to discipline me. On the weekend, instead of going to our cousins, we started going to our friends' house from school that we knew when Mama was alive. One in particular was Caroleen; her dad made home-brew beer, and he would let us have a drink of it. One day when we were there, Daddy drove up in his truck with a police car following him. He told the police to take us to juvenile hall. That was how he disciplined us for our bad behavior. We had to stay in there for a week. In my cell, there was a young lesbian that I had to share the cell with. She used to watch me the entire time even when I went to the bathroom. The toilet was in the cell with us. My dislike for my dad grew even more. It was a love-hate relationship. I wanted his love, but I hated him for the way he treated me. Whenever my dad was not happy with me, he would tell me that I was going to be just like my mother. He said that she was lazy and fat and just lay around all the time. I hated him for that. I couldn't believe that he was too ignorant to understand that Mama was sick, that the cancer wouldn't let her be who she wanted to be. Her large stomach was filling with tumors, and with nothing much else to eat except starches, the weight came. I knew that she couldn't work anymore; why couldn't he have seen the truth? He would always compare me with my sister Patsy who was quiet and very slender. She did well in school. I wasn't Patsy. I was who I was and couldn't be anyone else. I am not sorry that I didn't fit into his mold, but I do wish that he could have seen the talent for art and design that God placed in me. I lost myself once, and by the grace of God, I won't let anyone do that to me again. I have to be me. God has helped me to forgive my Dad for the verbal abuse that he used on me to try to control me. He hurt me so much. I don't know which is worse: the rapes from my brother or from the other teen boys and young men or the verbal abuse from my dad. It all messes you up on the inside in your head and spirit. I tried to make sure that I never told my children that they weren't any good or that I wished that they were like someone else. If I had, I ask them to forgive me now. After reading this story about my life, it may cause my own children to feel shame and embarrassment of me as their mother, having these things happen to me. To them, this I say, don't judge me, pray for me. You were not there. I know that it is not easy to forgive, but God will help you if you ask him. Someone once said that sin will take you farther than you want to go, make you pay more than you want to pay, and make you stay longer than you want to stay; and at the end, it will kill you. It causes physical death that leads to spiritual death. When you are made to feel like trash, you act like trash. Your parents can never give back what you feel was taken from you, only God can. Just as those people and my brother that hurt me can never pay me back, when I sow the hurt to God as seed, He will repay me. He will give joy for sorrow; He will turn the trashed life into a treasured life. I believe that my children and grandchildren will be great and do great things in their lives. If they will let Jesus be the Lord over their lives, they will be the head and not the tail, the first and not the last. God has a perfect plan for their lives. Even if you have missed it for years, He knows how to get you back on track if you yield your life to him. I am not going to try to pretend that I was the perfect parent to my children, because I wasn't. There was too many things that I wasn't able to give them; not tangible things like clothes, money, toys, things—they had that. I didn't know how to hug them and let them know that I loved them. I didn't even know how to encourage them in saving and being loyal to one another. I wish that I had encouraged my children to be the best in school and in everything that they put their hands to, to do. You can't do what you don't know. I didn't know how to encourage them to reach for God's best for themselves while they were growing up, but I do know how to pray for them now.

I speak a blessing over my children and grandchildren, and I would encourage you to bless yours as well. I say that they are prosperous in every area of their lives, and everything that they put their hands to will prosper, that they have favor with man and with God. They are blessed going in and blessed going out, blessed in the city and blessed in the field; that they will have houses and land in this life as well as the life to come, that riches and wealth will be in their homes. They shall be taught of the word of God and have great peace, and they shall live and not die early deaths. That they shall serve the Lord all the days of their lives. I say that every demonic spirit that has been assigned over their lives is bound from operating in their lives on earth as well as in heaven. I pray that the words of their mouths be acceptable in God's sight. I say that they have to love one another and that they esteem one another more highly than themselves. I pray all in the precious name of Jesus. Amen, so be it. I also ask that you forgive your fathers on earth for whatever they did or didn't do as well as your mothers because holding unforgiveness will keeping you from God's forgiveness. Jesus said in his word: "But if you do not forgive others their trespasses [their reckless and willful sins], leaving them, letting them go, and giving up resentment, neither will your Father [in heaven] forgive you your trespasses." By the time I was thirteen, I was well on my way to being an alcoholic. We lived in a small town and because of the time we lived in, we could buy beer and cigarettes and malt liquor at the store for our parents. They never asked whom it was for. I would steal money from my dad's wallet to buy the beer, *True Confessions* magazines, and comic books to read, and personal items. He didn't give us an allowance. I don't know how he expected us to get the things that young teenage girls needed. He might have known that we were taking money out of his wallet because he started hiding it. He would move it from one hiding place to another. I would always find it; the house didn't have too many hiding places in it. It was a big house, but there was hardly any furniture in it or hiding places. Just the necessary things, beds: couch kitchen table, and our clothes hanging in the closets. If you shoved them together, there would probably be two feet of clothing in a fourteen-foot closet. He had plenty of clothes; he had really nice expensive suits for church and nice shiny shoes. All we had was the radio, our magazines, and funny books, such as Super Man, Wonder Woman, Fantastic Four, and so on. We were stuck between being children and adults with no guidance. Once when I was coming home from cutting school, I took a shortcut across a deserted section of land, about ten acres. Some of the bad boys that had dropped out of school saw me and pulled a knife on me. They forced me to go into the old abandoned house on the property. There were about six boys, and they all forced themselves on me, dragging me like an old discarded sack on the floor of the old house through glass from broken windows. I had scars for years on my body from the glass that I lay on and which cut me. When they were finished with me, I had to walk the rest of the way home dirty and with dry blood on my clothes and body. I was only fourteen; some of them were between seventeen and twenty years of age. You young men and older men too, you think that you are getting your satisfaction and that you are just sowing your wild oats when you have sex with anyone. What you don't realize is that you are also destroying your own lives as well as the women and girls that you are having sex with that are not your wives. The Bible says in Genesis that "a man shall leave his father and mother and shall be come united and cleave to his wife, and they shall become one flesh." When you join yourself with someone else, you sin against your own flesh. You are becoming one with that person, you will always carry a spiritual part of them with you. Proverbs 6:32 says, "But whoever commits adultery with a woman lacks heart and understanding [moral principle]. He who does it is destroying his own life." After that, they would lie in wait for me to be alone at different places and rape me. Once I was walking through the small baseball park, and they came up and dragged me into a baseball dugout and raped me. Red Bluff was a small town, and where we lived, we had to walk pretty much everywhere we went, especially if we weren't old enough to have a car to get around. Several times, some of them would come up on motorcycles as I was walking and make me get on; they would take me out in the country on a path off of the road and rape me. By this time, I was so desensitized that I would succumb to their whims. I just got on the motorcycle. I knew that if I didn't, they would force me to get on anyway. They would take me out into the country into a cluster of trees and rape me, three or four boys at a time. I saw myself as nothing, just trash to be used and discarded. Tears again, cleansing tears. Maybe I went through this so that I could help someone else to get healed from his or her ordeal. I don't know. Sometimes I think that I know why Mary, the one that was said to be a harlot in the Bible, loved Jesus so. When you have succumbed to such evil and abuse in your life, you are grateful to the one that rescues you from such a life. I can imagine that after Jesus delivered her, the very next time one of the townsmen came to her seeking sexual favors, she was jubilant to be able to say no to them. I know that I was. Later on in my life, I too was able to say no, and they knew that I meant it. That was one of the most uplifting days of my life. God gives us the power to say no to sin. We can't just say *no* without power behind us to back it up. You don't just wake up from a great life and say, "I think that I am going to be a harlot or a prostitute today," or "I think I am going to murder someone or rob a bank or even molest someone." Circumstances, pain, and lack of love play a key part in the decisions that we make, along with Satan's deception. Some just make the choice to do evil. Even then, we don't know the consequences that we bring on ourselves by those decisions and choices that we make. The choices that we make now will catch up with us good or bad. This is where God's grace comes in; we deserve to reap what we sow, but if we accept that Jesus is the only begotten son of God who came to earth in human form and died for our sins on the cross, we will receive His grace (undeserved favor), and He will give us a new life. Jesus died, suffered unmercifully, and rose again for our past, present, and future sins. I thought that I would be really angry when I came to this part of writing about my life. For years, I carried hatred for those young men. I wanted them to burn in hell for the things that they had done to me, but now, I am calm while writing about this unfortunate time in my life. God has healed my spirit to the point that I pray somehow they found Christ before they died. Yes, I said died. Almost every one of them died an early death; others are on drugs, and their lives are a mess. Some were killed; some died with diseases or heart attacks and of drugs. I pray that they somehow found Christ and accepted Him as their savior, because now I realize that it is Satan that deceives people into thinking that they are immortal, that they can do harm to others and not have to pay the piper. The word of God says that you will reap what you sow, good or evil. I also know that these were someone's children. I know that one of them had a pastor for a father. Maybe someone prayed for them; I know that someone prayed for me. Satan has a plan for your life just as God has a plan for your life. Most of us have seen the old cartoons with the little devil sitting on one shoulder and the angel sitting on the other, whispering into someone's ears. If you only knew how true that really is. It was made to be a joke designed to blind us from the truth so that we laugh it off and not take it seriously. Satan studies your life from the time you are a baby. He learns what you like and what you don't like; what you like to look at, eat, hear; what feels good to us; and what we see (your senses), touch, feel, smell; and what you hear. These are what he uses against you to draw you away from the plan that God has for your life. He uses the pride of life and the lust of the eye, our fleshly desires or sensual pleasures, to entice us away or into something that will eventually cause us to fail.

Satan will bait you with a small taste of this thing or a small taste of that thing to see your reaction and how you respond to it. Maybe it is something that you have told yourself that you will never do. After the hook has been skillfully hidden behind the thoughts, he plants in your mind that "just a little won't hurt," "I'll just look at the picture of this naked woman one more time," "I'll just take a little sip of that drink to see what it tastes like," "One more cookie won't hurt," "I need something to calm me down." Soon it will change to "I need something to get me started." Then we find ourselves looking up from the bottom of a pit and wondering how we got there. The enemy then tries to make us too proud to cry out to God the Father who loves us and had the better plan for our lives. We think that we can fix it or get out ourselves, but Satan will make sure that you never do if he can help it. Please cry out to God now! Ask Him to help you; He will hear you. Another thing that Satan will do is to make you believe that you are not as bad as someone else is. That your sin is not as bad as their sin is. Most of us believe that we are not bad people, but God has set the Ten Commandments in to play for us to judge ourselves. Without the law, we wouldn't know that we are sinners; without Grace, we couldn't know forgiveness. Have you ever used the Lord's name in vain or looked on a man or woman with lust? Oh, you say you don't lust. Really. Have you ever had someone of the opposite sex smile at you and say something nice to you, and just for a moment you find yourself trying to stand a little prouder or say something slick or cute so they will desire you. Maybe even try to look just a little bit more sexy. You can actually feel that spirit trying to manipulate you. If you steal a nickel, what are you? You are a thief. If you tell one lie, you are a liar. It is the same as saying, "I am just a little pregnant." Jesus Christ died for our sins, and He is the only one that can reconcile you to God. If any man tries to come to God any other way, he is a thief and a robber. Thieves will not have a place in heaven without the blood of Jesus covering their sin. All have come short of the glory of

God. God wants to help you, but you have to ask Him. In the lives of these young men or my brother, maybe someone took something from them when they were young so they learned to take. Maybe they were molested as a young child and so learned to molest someone else. It is passed from generation to generation. This is what is known as generational curses. If you ever notice in different families, there are certain things that seem to be passed on from generation to another. Satan has assigned evil spirits over different families. You may see that the grandfather, the son, and the grandson all were alcoholics, or that there were a lot of suicides and tragic deaths in a family line, or promiscuity, family members on drugs, and so on. Unless one turns to God to stop the curse from being passed down to each generation in their family, it will continue. He will make you in right standing with him. He will make you the righteousness of God by His son Christ Jesus. If you confess your sins, God is faithful and just to forgive us our sins. God already knows what you did or thought; he just wants you to acknowledge it to Him. When someone hurts you, it takes God's help to be able to forgive him or her, especially when all you want to do is get even with them or send them straight to hell. When someone hurts you, as I was hurt, only God can give you the strength to forgive or even the love to want to. That person is someone's child and God loves him or her, just as much as he loves you. You may feel that if you forgive them that they have gotten away with what they did. But they don't get away. God said that vengeance is His, and he will repay, and He does. He also tries to get them to turn from their evil ways. When we release them to Him, then He can start His work. God's word also said that if we are glad and we rejoice when we see our enemies destroyed or reaping what they have sown, it would be worse for us than what they did to us in the first place. God wants us to be free to live our lives. Unforgiveness will not allow us to be free. That is why He wants us to give it over to Him to take care of as only he can. To prevent the hoodlum gang from bothering me anymore, I got a boyfriend; actually, he was a man-friend. Before I found a steady boyfriend, I started going out with other young men that were in their early to midtwenties. We would sit around talking while they worked on their cars. Anybody that was somebody had a car that they worked on, on weekends—probably a '53 or '56 Chevy or Cadillac or Buick car. When they were finished putting whatever it was that they were putting in the car that day, we would go for a ride in the country. Most of the time we would end up in the back seat or on a dirty blanket. I don't think that I even cared anymore by this time. I had lost respect for myself. It wasn't about a feeling, it was just something you did. And then when it was over, the shame that you feel is overwhelming, knowing that you mean absolutely nothing to them. When you feel as low and as dirty as you have ever felt, remember that Christ can wash you and make you cleaner than you ever felt. After a year or so, I met Eddie. Eddie was twenty-two and I had just turned fifteen. I would go to his place and we would drink Galo, Vin Rosa wine and watch TV all day. On the weekends and some weekdays that he didn't go to work, on these days, I cut school and stayed with him until it would be time for me to come home from school. Then I would leave for home. He was already an alcoholic. I never saw him so drunk that he would be falling down or stumbling, but he always had a glass or bottle of wine in his hand, with glassy-looking eyes. The only thing that I cared about was that he treated me decent. Patsy and I would sneak out of the window at night to go meet our boyfriends. Sometimes Satan still tries to make me feel guilty for leading my younger sister into such things, even though I have asked her to forgive me, and I have asked God to forgive me too. I was supposed to be taking care of her, not bringing harm to her. Once I had cut school and had been drinking with Eddie; I was so drunk it was a wonder that I made it home. I always walked most of the way home so that Daddy wouldn't know that I had been with him. I was walking down the side of the highway toward home when my dad came up the road in his truck on his way home from his job. He stopped and asked if I wanted a ride, and I told him no, that I was trying to get some exercise or something, I don't remember. I couldn't tell you what I said, but I got immediately sober for the thirty seconds or so that I was talking to him. As soon as he drove off, the world started spinning again. I don't know how he couldn't have smelled the liquor on me or even realized that I was coming from the wrong direction to be coming from school. I never thought that he cared about me one way or another anyway, and had told him so on one occasion when he had bashed me with degrading talk. Now I am sure that he did; he just didn't know what to do or how to show he cared.

Eddie was fun to be with for a while, but he was getting too serious, and it scared me. I hadn't had anyone really care about me before that I was aware of. I know that he really liked me, maybe even loved me. After we had dated for several months, he went to my dad and asked him to let him marry me one day when I was at school. When I came home from school, on one of the few days that I went then, my dad told me that Eddie had come over to talk to him about marrying me. I couldn't believe that he would come to the house and ask Daddy to marry me. The crazy thing was that Daddy had told him that I could marry him. I was only fifteen and Eddie was already twenty-three. I told Daddy that I wasn't marrying him. I stopped going out with Eddie because I didn't want to get married. I never saw him after that, but when I asked someone several years later, they told me that he had died from liver failure and alcoholism. To me, my dad saying that I should marry Eddie was the next thing to people selling their daughters off to someone like a lot of the people overseas give their daughters to someone for a herd of goats, a dowry, or money. When I see how some of the young girls are used for sex and are drugged and beaten for not performing sex, it breaks my heart. That is why I give to ministries that help to free these young girls. Some of the women have had children that are held captive as well. My dad, being so much older when he had children, I suppose that it was perfectly fine with him to have me marry at fifteen. When he was young, the girls married young. I didn't want to get married. What I had seen of marriage was not the best example. My dad had been married before he was with my mom, and I knew that Mama and Daddy hadn't been married. I also saw that the woman that he did marry after my mama left him hated kids. Why someone would marry a man with two children knowing that they didn't like children is beyond me. Maybe because we lived with my mom she thought that she wouldn't have to deal with us. My dad and his wife even slept in different bedrooms. And remember, my dream was to be a kept woman, not to get married. I was going to somehow find a rich man and be his mistress, and Eddie was by no means rich, so I made myself unavailable to him. After we broke up, I discovered that I was pregnant. I didn't know that I was, but one morning before school, my stomach was hurting really bad and I thought that I had the flu or something. Maybe I had food poisoning again. I had eaten some liver once when we first moved to my dad's place that had given me food poisoning. I thought that I was surely going to die, my stomach hurt so bad. It left me weak and sore after two days. When I went to the bathroom, this thing fell out of me into the toilet. It didn't come from where my stool comes out. It came out of my private area. I didn't know what the heck it was. I didn't know anything about getting pregnant although Eddie and I had sexual relations sometimes. I had seen a film at school in junior high about a sperm fertilizing an egg, but I'll be dogged if I knew what the sperm really came from and how it got into you. At school, they just showed it floating through the air and then touch each other. What did that have to do with sex? When the fetus plopped into the toilet, I was so scared. With my imagination and reading comic books with weird space creatures, I could only imagine that some monster had crawled up inside of me and was coming out. I didn't know if there was more in me or not. Here was another situation that I didn't know what to do with. I looked into the toilet to see what it was. The water had washed off some of the blood, and I could tell it was some kind of creature. I know now that it was an undeveloped baby, but at the time, it looked like some kind of alien baby monster. It was about three inches long, the arms and legs were not formed, and the head was almost as large as the body. It looked like something that I have seen in a jar in a science-fiction movie. After standing there looking at it for a long while, I fished it out of the toilet and studied it. I decided that it was forming into a baby, but it was so ugly I was afraid of it, so I wrapped it up in some paper towels. I put it into my purse and got dressed for school, all the while wondering what to do. When I got to school, I put it into my locker and went to class, still afraid and anxious of what to do with it. There was no way that I could know what the teacher was saying that day in class. At lunchtime, I went back to the locker. We had some early warm summer days and it smelled in my locker when I opened the door, so I took it out and put it into the trash can. I know that it was dead; it never moved at all when it came out of me. I have never forgotten it though.

CHAPTER

5

I needed to get away from all of the crazy things that were happening to me, so I ran away. I had fallen into such a pit of low self-esteem that I had decided to use my own body to get me out of the mess that I was in. I had read in the *True Confessions* books how the prostitutes made money with their bodies, so I thought that I would try it. It seemed that everybody else was using me for something, I might as well use myself too. I put a few clothes in a brown paper bag and went looking for this old man that liked young girls. In small towns, everybody knows what's going on with everybody else. For a favor, he gave me the money to buy a bus ticket to Sacramento. I was trying to find my brother. I don't know why, but I was hoping that he would help me. As I have said, you try to push your past hurts into the parts of your mind that you hope will hide them and make you forget, so I didn't think about our past. When I got the money, I bought a bus ticket to Sacramento. Sacramento was so much bigger than Red Bluff. I wasn't sure where to go, but I remember Buddy saying that he lived in Oak Park. I had walked from downtown to old Tower Theatre on Broadway Boulevard with my three-inch heels. I asked someone where Oak Park was and found that I still had a ways to go. I was tired and hungry. While I was standing outside of the Tower Theatre a well-dressed man in a nice car pulled up to the curb and asked me if I needed a ride. Because I was low in money, I decided that I could earn some more money since I knew that was want the man really wanted. You get to know who people are just by the spirit they give off. After all, I was just a piece of trash on the sidewalk waiting to be picked up by someone. When we left the motel on Stockton Boulevard, he dropped me off on a corner in Oak Park, not knowing that it wasn't far from where my brother actually lived. Walking down one street, I asked people that I met if they knew Buddy Earl. In Red Bluff, most everybody know everyone else in town. I don't know how I found him, but I did. He told me that I needed to go back home because he didn't have anywhere for me to stay. I found one of my aunts in Sacramento who had moved there a few years earlier. Mama had told me she was my godmother. Aunt Sherry let me stay with her a couple of nights but then told me that I needed to go back home too. Maybe if I would have told her what was going on in my life in Red Bluff she would have let me stay, but it wasn't to be so at this time. Most of my other aunts and family believed that I was just a wild child and they didn't want, or have the time or energy, to deal with me. They were unaware of the rapes and molestation that had gone on in my life. What would happen to Patsy when I left hadn't crossed my mind when I left; I was just trying to get away from my life. I knew that I needed to go back to help her to get away. When I got back to Red Bluff, the same kinds of things started again: the rapes and molestation. After another few months, I ran away again. This time, I took Patsy with me. I stole a couple of twenties out of my dad's wallet for our tickets. There were pimps waiting around the bus station in Sacramento looking for young girls to use and put on the street. One such man said that we could stay with him, and he took us to his house. We didn't have any food or money left, so we went with him. He lived in a shabby boarding house downtown. The place was one big room divided into a living area, a kitchenette, and on the other end of it he had hung a sheet to divide the space into two-bedroom areas and finally the bathroom at the very end to one side. He gave Patsy and me the bed on one side and he had the bed on the other side. If you were on one side of the sheet, you could hear everything that was going on, on the other side of it. He told me to come into the side where he was and get into the bed. When I went around the sheet, I stopped and looked back. I didn't want Patsy to know what was happening although I am sure that she did. He put a gun to my head and made me have sex with him. All I could think about was that Patsy was right there almost in the same room. It made me sick to my stomach. I didn't know what he would do to Patsy if we stayed there. I had to find a way to get her out of there. I thought that I was protecting her by taking her with me, but I had just made things worse. I can't even began to tell you the guilt that I felt by bringing Patsy into this situation. Guilt that weighed me down so much that I couldn't breathe whenever I allowed myself to think about it. It put a knot in my stomach and brought tears to my eyes every time that Satan brought it to my memory. The next day after we ate breakfast, he told me that it was time for me go out and find a John and make some money. I didn't want to leave Patsy there with him. The only thing that I could do was to hope that he thought that she was too young to mess with, so I left and walked the few blocks back toward the bus station. I wanted to find someone that would pay me to have sex with them fast so that I could get back to Patsy. After about an hour, I did find someone willing to pay. Although I had made some money, I could never see myself giving any money that I made with my body to some man. I hid the money and after another hour, I went back and told him that I couldn't find anyone that wanted to buy sex. When he went out the next day to take care of business, Patsy and I left. I was afraid that we might run into him on the way to the bus station. I used some of the money to get a bus ticket to send Patsy back home. I had brought her into danger trying to protect her. I had made things worse for her. After I put her on a bus back to Red Bluff, I walked the street trying to figure out what to do. For years, I carried the guilt that I had done by bringing Patsy with me to that pimp's place. Every time I thought about it, my stomach would knot up in anguish and guilt. There were times that I didn't want to face her. Some years ago, I finally asked her to forgive me for leading her into the messes that I had gotten us in. Her quick response was that she already had. But I couldn't forgive myself. One night, I woke up while still in the process of writing this book. The thought of me taking Patsy with me when I ran away became heavy on my mind. My stomach began to churn and knot up again when a still small voice from the Holy Spirit spoke to my spirit and set me free once and for all. I said earlier that God also gave us another gift, that gift is the Holy Spirit. He is our comforter, teacher, our guide, and very present help in the time of need. He reminded me that in Isaiah 53:5, "He [meaning Jesus] was wounded for our transgressions, He was bruised for our guilt *and* iniquities; the chastisement [needful to obtain] peace *and* well-being for us was upon Him, and with the stripes [that wounded] Him we are healed *and* made whole." By faith I received my salvation through Christ, and by faith, I needed to receive that He was bruised for my guilt. When the Holy Spirit spoke those words into my spirit and I received them, all of the pain and guilt was instantly removed from me. God is a good God. You too can be free from guilt that Satan uses to hold your mind captive, to hold you down and keep you from moving forward in life.

I was used to my body being used by men now, so I figured if someone else could use it, I could too. I went to a room with a man that was looking for a good time. We drank a bottle of alcohol. He wasn't aware that I was used to drinking at a young age, but evidently he wasn't. When he got so drunk that he fell asleep, I stole the money out of his wallet. I had taken it all out, but my conscience made me leave him a twenty-dollar bill. I was used to drinking probably more than a lot of men were by then. I could drink a half-gallon of wine and not get sloppy drunk. When I ran out of money, I tried to find another John. This time the guy pulled a knife on me after he got what he wanted and made me get out of the car. I roamed the street that night and slept in a seat in the Greyhound bus station. Although I was on the street as a prostitute for a very short time, it was long enough for me to know what a lot of the women have to go through with pimps and on their own. Getting beat and hit, men using your body as a battering ram because they hate women and are taking their frustrations out on you. No matter if it is one man or two hundred and one or more requires God's healing touch. I don't care how you wash yourself and scrub until your skin bleeds. He (God) is the only one that can wash you whiter than snow. After God saved me, I had a truck driver try to proposition me. I told him that I had discovered a new way; this got his interest and curiosity. Then I told him about Jesus Christ, how he is the way and the life. I also prayed for his salvation. Only God can make us new creations in Christ Jesus, just as if we never sinned. We can be spiritual virgins for our husbands, and our husband can be our first, as mine is for me. I am blessed to have a husband that is aware of what happened in my past life to a certain extent. But you must be led by Holy Spirit if you intend to tell your husband or wife about your past. There are also men that have been abused and misused. Some have been turned out to prostitution and homosexuality. God loves you too. You are judged by what you do with Jesus Christ. You don't need to try to fix yourself. Give your life to Christ and ask Him to do whatever needs to be done in your life. That is *grace*. The law tells you to work to do something; Grace does it for you when you cast your cares on Him. Christ is Grace. People get discouraged trying to change themselves. Put God's word in your heart and mouth by reading His word and be patient; He will begin to change what needs to be changed. A lot of men cannot take it that their wife has been raped and molested. The word of God says only a fool utters all of his mind. And if you do plan on telling them at all, you might want to do it before you get married because you could be looking at a divorce. If they can't accept you as you are, they may not be a good candidate to marry. They have to believe that you are a new creature in Christ Jesus and not hold your past before you. I didn't say against you, because some people will bring it up, constantly holding it in front of you to make you feel guilty so that they can play on your guilt. The next day, I eventually found another guy wanting a young girl for some fun on the side. He said that his wife was looking for a babysitter and that he would talk to her about letting me live with them and take care of the kids. I can't tell you all the things that I went through before I found the family to stay with the next day. The things you go through to survive aren't always pretty. What I will tell you is that I had guns and knives pulled on me. I had gone from one kind of hell to another. It didn't matter where I went; it seemed to follow me everywhere. So I deadened myself to the abuse. This was not how life was supposed to be. When you read these pages, you may judge me and feel that I didn't have to be where I was, but I didn't know any other way. Yes, I could have stayed in Red Bluff and just gone to school and locked myself in the house, but some of the guys had started coming to my dad's house when they saw him leave for work. These young men preyed on girls that had no protection or brothers to help them. I had no one to turn to but myself. You see, I didn't know that God would love or help someone like me. Someone else may have even tried to kill themselves in this situation, but God kept me with a heart to survive, and survive I did. He was with me even then. While I was standing outside of the Greyhound bus station, I saw this guy driving by looking at me. When I saw him make the block and come back around, I knew that I had a taker. He said that his wife was looking for child care, and we devised a plan that if his wife agreed, I would stay with them and watch their kids and do favors for him since he was doing this so-called favor for me. He told his wife that a friend of his recommended me and said that I would be a good live-in babysitter for them. What he didn't tell her was that in return, I was to do favors for him while his wife was at work. I needed a place to live temporarily, so I hardened my heart and did what I needed to survive. This went on for several months; the thing that happened to end it was that his wife had a brother that I had met, and after a few months we started dating. I really liked him, so when her husband tried to have sex with me after a few months' time, I told him that I wouldn't have sex with him anymore because I was dating his wife's brother. I called Allen to come over because Ely wouldn't leave me alone, but a few days later he tried, to get me to have sex with him again. I had told Allen about what I had been doing with Ely and that I had told him to leave me alone. When Ely tried to force himself on me, I ran and called Allen and told him what he tried to do. Allen came over to the house with a baseball bat and told him that he had better never touch me again. For the first time, I felt that someone loved me, that someone really cared about me; he was the first teenage boy that I could talk to. It wasn't hard falling in love with him. He was a smooth-talker and knew just what a girl wanted to hear. This was how his wife found out about what had been going on between her husband and me. She was a Christian and forgave me. She let me stay on at her house for a while. I know that she was really saved or crazy; for one thing, there is no way that I would have let anyone still live at my house after that. Number two, I would have kicked their behind for them after giving them food and a place to live and they do this to me. I have had people to tell me to leave their home after telling them part of my story. Allen was the first male that I really loved outside of my dad. Allen treated me special; we would go for walks to the park and talk about school and life in general. I had enrolled back into school when I moved in with Ellen and her husband. Since she worked at night, it worked out for both of us. I attended school for a few months, but by the time the end of school came, I found myself in another mess. Being teenagers and wanting to have fun on the last day of school, someone had bought a bottle of rum to school. There were about eight of us sitting at a table in the school cafeteria with sodas in cups. We all shared a little of the rum in our cups. I was use to drinking wine, but I had never had rum before.

I want to interject here that if you have ever been raped and made to feel ashamed to report it to the police, you should by all means report it. Do not let anyone intimidate you. It may not only save someone else's life but also help to free you from the violation. There are men that would say in a court of law that you enjoyed it so that it wasn't rape. I want you to know that a woman's body was made to react to stimulation in certain areas. God created sex to be enjoyed, but enjoyed by a husband and wife. There are women that feel shame because when they are being raped, that after the act went on for a few minutes, their bodies begin to respond to being violated. Please, please don't allow the enemy to use that on you. For so many decades, women were used and given over to the whims of men; even some husbands abused their own wives. I am sure that you have heard men say, "She likes it rough," so they feel that being abusive to a woman is all right because her body begins to respond after a while of being pillaged. Women want to be loved. We are the weaker creatures when it comes to being physical.

Women were not created to be rammed and jabbed; it will eventually cause damage to our female organs, or cancer. I know it was God that finally got it over to judges of the court that because a woman's body responded during rape that it should be constituted as rape. Too many woman were hurt and defamed because people didn't understand the psyche and makeup of the female body, and there is still too many that don't understand it today, both men and women themselves. Allen and I continued dating and going to school. I felt like a normal teen, enjoying my life and boyfriend, one of my age group finally. On the last day of school, there was a group of us sitting together in the school cafeteria. Someone had bought a bottle of rum to celebrate it being the last day of school, and we all brought sodas in cups from the vending machine and put a little rum in with the soda. Just being teens having fun with our secret. After drinking some soda with alcohol in it, I had to use the bathroom and left my drink on the table with so-called friends. When I returned, I drank the rest of my drink. By now the bell was ringing to go back to class after lunch. By the time I reached the hall leading to my class, I could hardly stand up. Someone had put more than rum in my drink while I was gone. I found myself stumbling and clawing my way down the brick hallway. I thought that I needed to go outside and get fresh air. When I reached the door leading outside, a male voice asked me if I wanted to sit in his car and rest a minute. I could barely see where I was going. After I fell heavily into the car, I discovered that there was more than one male in the car. I was just too weak to get back out. Someone had drugged my drink when I went to the bathroom, most likely one of these teens. It was the date-rape drug that was used so commonly in the late sixties. By now I could only hear voices. When I tried to open my eyes, I could only see blurred images. There were several other teenaged boys in the car that had not been in it earlier. I could hear different voices, and I did recognize one distinct voice belonging to someone I knew. I heard them say that they were taking me to the park. They all took turns with my body. Several hours later, the police found my almost lifeless body thrown under some bushes at the park. I don't know if someone saw me or a neighbor saw them and called the police or what, but I may have died if I had been left there. Again, this reinforced the idea to me that I wasn't worth much to be just thrown away like some discarded trash. I suppose that I had my school ID on me because they found the family that I had been living with and took me there. Ellen gave me a cold shower and put me to bed. She thought that I was drunk but found out later that I had been drugged. She told me when I finally woke up that I had been asleep for two days. A couple of months before my ordeal with the drugs, Ely had left me alone so Allen and I had been enjoying our time together. We would go fishing with Ellen and her husband and just walk off to ourselves holding hands. A couple of times we were alone and made love, I didn't know about using protection, so needless to say, eventually, I got pregnant; but I didn't know that I was. I was going to school getting my education. I enjoyed babysitting for Ellen's children; they were like my little sisters and brothers to me. I missed my sisters, so they helped to occupy my time when Allen wasn't around. I would read and play ball with them and play with them in their little wading pool in the summer. Allen confessed his love for me, so for me, life couldn't have been better at the time. We both planned to go to college and make a life for ourselves. It was a few weeks later that I discovered that I was pregnant. Ellen let me stay on babysitting after school was out for the summer until she discovered that I was pregnant, then she sent me packing. One day she was making homemade chili and I got sick to my stomach; a week later, she made some spaghetti, and I almost puked my guts out. With her being a nurse, she knew the signs. When she told me that I was pregnant, I told her that I wasn't. I really didn't know it at the time. I thought that I had the flu or something. She asked if I had my cycle that month and I couldn't remember. It was all over the Heights that I had a train pulled on me the last day of school—that is what they call a gang rape—and for this reason, Allen said that the baby was not his. I supposed that he blamed me for getting drugged. I tried to persuade him that it was his baby before I left. I knew that I wouldn't be able to after I left. I did the math; I had to have been pregnant before they raped me. But I knew once that I left, people would put all sorts of ideas in his head, and they did. When I got back home, I told my dad that I was pregnant. He just looked at me, didn't even give a response. The next day, he went to the bank drew out some money and gave me fifty dollars. He told me to pack some clothes and took me back to the bus station. He told me to go back to Sacramento and tell the boy to marry me. Ha! That was a laugh. I mean you can't just go tell somebody to marry you just because your dad tells you to. I would love to have married him if I could have. I loved Allen. But now I am ever grateful that I didn't marry him; time has shown a different side to him. What I did was take the money and catch the bus back to Sacramento, but I wasn't going to ask anyone to marry me. I stayed with my Aunt Jenny, who had also moved to Sacramento by this time, for a couple of days. I used the money to go to the state fair that was going on at the time to help me feel better, but it didn't. After I spent the money, I went back to Red Bluff. I did try to convince Allen that it was his baby before I left town, but I couldn't change his mind. I returned to Red bluff with my heart throbbing. I cried just as much over him as I did just a few years earlier when my mother died. Every time a song came on the radio that we had shared together, I would cry. I would cry just when I thought of him. I cried until I didn't have tears to cry. I couldn't really blame Allen; I probably would have done the same thing if I were in his place. For some reason in that time, and still some today, if a girl or woman is raped, it is believed to have been her fault somehow. That is one of the biggest lies going. It was designed to cause the woman even more self-loathing and self-condemnation. I began sneaking out of the window at night again, going to parties that someone gave until my stomach started getting in the way. Then I just stayed at home until my baby was born. I didn't want to go visit the few friends in Red Bluff that I had before I left because I had heard that some people had been talking about me anyway. You were considered a slut if you got pregnant and wasn't married. Although things that had been done in the dark with some family members has since come out in the light, but at that time when they thought that their secrets were safe, I was the talk of the town. I had turned sixteen five months before I had my baby. I loved him so much; he seemed to be the only one that needed me. I had taken home economics as a freshman in high school and had learned to sew. I made him little outfits that no other baby would have. I made him a little blue-and-white-striped sailor suit and matching shorts and tops. Sometimes I would change him four or five times a day just to see what he looked like in a different outfit. I spoiled him in the day, sometimes just holding him and looking at him. He was like a little doll. I knew that he would grow up and love me and I would love him. I named him Allen Gerone. My spoiling him in the daytime didn't make matters better for me at night. Gerone was born in the spring, but by the time the end of May came around, it was getting pretty hot. Daddy had never let us use an air conditioner before and just because I had Gerone things did not change. The house was so hot that perspiration would form on your body even if you just lay still on the bed. Gerone was fussy most of the day (I called him by his middle name). After a couple of weeks of him fretting all the time, Daddy made me walk him up and down the hallway at night every time; he just grunted in his sleep. He could hear him whimper in his sleep through the heating and air vents in the ceiling that we couldn't use. My baby had gotten so spoiled that I had to sleep with him on my stomach. He developed heat rash that made him more uncomfortable. Needless to say, I was worn out, and with the lack of sleep and heat I didn't know what to do. After Gerone was born, my dad bought a half-acre parcel of land that was next door to his house; he also bought a two-bedroom used trailer to put on it for Gerone and me to live in. When I look back at the things that he did do for me and tried to help me in his own way, he tried to be a good dad but didn't know how to show his love. He just didn't know the first thing about raising children, especially girls. There was no way that I was going to move into that trailer knowing what would eventually happen with the gang of boys that lived in the small town. Unfortunately after two months, I finally packed up my bags and left home for good. I had started getting welfare checks for us although I wasn't aware that they had finally started coming until two months after they started. My dad was getting my checks and cashing them. When I asked if he had seen a check come in the mail with my name on it, he said that he thought that they were paying him for jury duty. With us having the same initials, he had been cashing my checks since they only had my initials and last name, which was the same as his. He never offered to pay it back after he found out. I guess he figured that I owed him for the money that I had stolen from his wallet before I left home. With the next check that I received, I used it to move back to Sacramento. When I moved back to Sacramento, I found out that Gerone's dad, Allen, had been dating someone else at the same time that he was dating me and had another baby by someone else around the same age as Gerone. I think that they were only a month apart. I couldn't believe that he accused me of cheating on him when he was the one doing the cheating. I stayed with my Aunt Jenny for a few days until I found a studio apartment. The first thing I did was to put my baby down in the middle of the full-sized bed and put pillows down on the floor. I made sure he was changed and fed and let him yell until he cried himself to sleep. After that one time, he would go to sleep without me laying him on my stomach or having to hold him and rock him to sleep, and I could finally get some rest. He was a good baby; I had just never been allowed to train him as long as I was living with my dad. Actually, all of my babies were good sleepers after a few weeks. A couple of months later, I met a really nice guy I started dating, I don't know what really happened between us, but it didn't last. I met up with Allen, Gerone's dad, again and he still said that Gerone wasn't his after looking at him. I don't know who he would think that a two-month-old baby would look like; his features weren't developed yet. He said that Gerone didn't look like him nevertheless. Gerone has my nose, which is somewhat a pug, and his dad's is more Indianlooking. Although after Gerone became a teen, he looked as though Allen spit Gerone out, as the older folks used to say.

I hadn't had contact with my family since I left Red Bluff, and I was wondering how Patsy was doing. After stopping by my Aunt Jenny's one day, she told me that Patsy had moved in with my Aunt Sherry here in Sacramento. I was so glad that she was able to get away from

Red Bluff. I still didn't know how Rita was getting along. I hadn't heard from her in over a year. Her dad had married a woman that would hardly let her communicate with us. When Rita did get a letter to us, we wrote back asking if she had gotten our letters because she never mentioned the things in the letter that we had inquired about. Later I discovered that her stepmother had been really mean to her and hadn't given her half of our letters. I tried to get one of my aunts to take her, but they couldn't get her from her legal father and stepmother without going to court and proving them unfit. None of them was willing to do that or knew how to prove it. They had brought Rita to visit once in three years since my mom had passed, before I left Red Bluff, and they would hardly ever let her be alone with us. Occasionally, I would visit my aunt Sherry to see my sister Patsy. I felt that she was safe now, so I didn't visit much because most of the time, she was at school; and by me riding the bus, I needed to make sure that I left her house at a certain time to make my connections to get back to the side of town that I lived on. After living in the studio apartment in Del Paso, I found a one-bedroom apartment and moved into it. Being a young inexperienced mother, I didn't know anything about how to budget the money that I received from welfare. There were times when my money got short and we didn't have quite enough food at the end of the month. I would go to the neighborhood store and steal some baby food for Gerone and lunch meat for myself. After a few months of running out of food, I learned how to budget my money, I learned how to pay my bills first and by groceries before I did any other kind of shopping. It was mostly just Gerone and I for almost a year. I took care of my baby the best that I knew how. I would visit Allen's adopted mom and aunts because they were mostly the only ones that I knew, besides my aunts and a few cousins. I didn't visit Allen's sister, but his adopted family and I got along well while we were dating, so I didn't see any reason to alienate them. Queen Ann, Ora Lee, and Mary Jo were all ways kind to me. I think I also hoped that I would see Allen there too. He did drop by once in a while, but he didn't say anything to me. I started hanging out with some of my guy cousins and some of their friends who lived in

Sacramento. I would go out to a party once in a while with them while Allen's adopted sister babysat Gerone. We would pile up into Robert's car and head for Oak Park looking for a party. The Black Panthers were big then, and everybody wanted to join the pack and go to their recruiting parties. They had the black lights and strobe lights going and all of the latest music going on. It was so dark in there no one knew if you could dance or not. Anyway, half of the time, most everybody just stood there, slow dancing and grinding. At that time, Oak Park was feuding with the Heights, so we would pretend that we were out of town when we went to the parties because we didn't want to get jumped on out of our territory. Around this time, I met my best friend Bertha Gray while living in the Heights. We both smoked menthol cigarettes that we thought made us look pretty hip, that was the word in the day. We dressed alike and went to parties together. Wearing our dashiki dresses, or polka-dot shirt-dresses. We would always share a bottle of wine just before we left for a party. The wine gave me a false sense of self-esteem. I believe that it did the same for Bertha; she was adopted by older parents and had a few issues also. It gave me the courage to dance a little. I didn't really know how to dance since I had never been asked to any dances at school in Red Bluff, but I quickly learned the new dances. I enrolled back in school, and Mary Jo would babysit for me. I would sometimes get sent home from school because I would wear my skirts too short. The hip-hugger and miniskirts were in. I loved my miniskirts and hip-hugging stovepipe pants sets with my belly showing my midriff. My preferred outfit would have been a mesh outfit with very little under it; sin makes you do foolish things. We would wear our Angela Davis Afros and big hoop earrings and black eye shadow with our go-go boots or platform shoes. There is no way you could tell me that I wasn't looking good then. With a baby, my dream of being a kept woman went out the window. I wanted to graduate high school and get a job. My best friend Bertha and I would buy the shirtdresses to wear to school, we both had a striped one and a blue one with yellow polka-dot shirt dress alike. I had finally begun feeling better about myself. Bertha was skinny as a bean, and we could wear the same size except for the shirtdresses. I had just a bit more hips after having Gerone now, and the button across my hips would pop out if I didn't get a size larger, but I knew that I was looking good with my natural and miniskirt. I went out with this guy named Raymond after I had started back to school, and we had sex; trust me, it wasn't love. Sometimes when you get used to being used, you just deaden your feelings and close your mind to what was going on just to have someone to be with you and not be alone. I had learned to just lie down to avoid the confrontation and arguments when I went out. I didn't enjoy having sex; it had just become a ritual when I went out. You hoped that you would find someone that wanted you for you, but it was always the same—they just wanted what they could get. So you block out your feelings and go with the flow. When it's over, you go on about your life as it is: looking for love in all the wrong places. Sometimes I would be disgusted with myself so much and swear that I won't do it again but I did. I guess with having been raped so many times and being with different men, someone had given me a venereal disease and I didn't know it. I don't know where it came from, but I am wondering why Allen never mentioned it. One day at lunchtime, Raymond came over to me at the little hamburger stand across the street from the school that we went to; he walked up to me and punched me in the eye with his fist. He said in front of everybody that I had given him a venereal disease. Embarrassed is not even the word that I would use; I was devastated. I went to the doctor to have it taken care of, but I didn't go out with anyone else in our school. That may have been why the other guy left me hanging and hadn't contacted me anymore, but he hadn't told me anything either, and I did like him. A few months later, I met an older guy that wasn't in my high school; he was about twenty-two. He asked me out to a dance that was held at a center down the street from the school. Since I hadn't been out for a while, I went with him. I had been out with older guys in Red Bluff that were in their twenties, so it didn't bother me that he was an older guy. We had a few drinks and danced for a while then he brought me home and dropped me off. I was happy that he was one of the first guys in a while that just wanted to go out and have fun and nothing more. After the dance, he dropped me off and left. I went on about my business as usual the next day and never thought about him anymore. I really wasn't interested in him. A couple of days later, I met Mr. Jamison Semore. My friend Bertha, who went to the same school as I did, had met this guy named Olli; he had two friends that he hung out with, Henry and Jamison (Bud). Jamison had asked Bertha if she had any girlfriends, and she told them about me. She brought them over to my apartment to meet me. We went joyriding in his grandmother's car since he didn't have his own. Later that evening after they left, Raymond came back over to my place with my cousin Robert and asked me if I wanted to go out again. I stepped out of the door as not to wake Gerone with our talking. I told him no, that I had met someone that I was interested in. He told my cousin that he wanted to talk to me alone. He told him that he wasn't going to do anything to me, that he just wanted to talk, so my cousin left me there with him. After he left, Raymond pulled out a gun and aimed it at my head. He forced me back into the apartment. He told me that no one breaks up with him. This was news to me; I didn't know that we were supposed to have been a couple. I had just gone out with him on a date, and with no sex. I told him that I had to leave and go somewhere, that I was late. He told me to go, but that I couldn't take my baby with me. There was no way that I was going anywhere and leave my baby with this crazy man. I didn't know what to do but did what he told me. I am thankful that Gerone was asleep through all of this. Raymond slapped me on both sides of my face, hard, and then forced himself on me. I lay there like a stone statue. He had the nerve to ask me if I liked it. I told him that I couldn't feel anything. When he had done what he wanted, he went outside and shot the gun up in the air. I wasn't afraid of dying. I believe that if he would have killed me that night that God would have saved my soul, but my baby needed me. I don't know why, but the night before, I had prayed the only prayer that I knew since I was a young girl; "If I should die before I wake, I pray the Lord my soul to take." I hadn't thought about praying before since I didn't think that it would be much good. I had heard Mama crying and praying out to God to help her, and she was gone. I am thankful for God's mercy. Again, I believe that God, in some small way, was letting me know that He was with me even through everything that I had done and went through. It was He who had put it into my heart to pray the night before. God's mercy is new every morning. Later on that night, my cousin came back and asked me what Raymond had wanted. I told him that he had pulled out a gun and shot it up in the air. I said that he was talking crazy, saying that nobody breaks up with him, and that I supposed that now, he felt that he broke up with me. That was a laugh. I didn't want to tell him the rest because I knew that my cousin was the kind of person that would go and confront him just for my honor and maybe get shot by that fool. The man was crazy and I had heard some years later that he had actually shot someone and gone to prison. I could have been the first on his list if it wasn't for God protecting me even though I didn't know it at the time. The next day, Jamison and his friends came back over. I tell you, by now, my mind was reeling. I didn't know if I wanted a boyfriend ever. I had nothing but problems with men. Jamison asked me who the guy was that I had gone out with. Now I'm wondering how he knew I had went out with Raymond. When I told him nobody, he hit me in the eye and gave me a black eye. What was this stuff anyway, men hitting me, giving me black eyes and going on? My mama didn't take no mess from my dad, and I wasn't taking no mess from another man. These weren't men anyway; these were boys—seventeen and eighteen—except Raymond, and I wasn't going to fight back with him and that gun. I told Jamison that he had better never put his hand on me again. I guess because I wanted to belong and have friends, I accepted his apology. After that, we all started hanging out together with his friends. Henry found himself another girl from the Heights that Bertha and I didn't hang with, so it was just Olli and Bertha and Jamison and myself. We would either be at my apartment or at Olli's apartment, drinking beer, smoking, and talking. Someone had started a rumor that I had taken Jamison from another girl that lived in the Heights. The girl and some of her friends all wanted to fight me. She got her friends to come to my apartment, and they broke out all my windows one day when I wasn't home. When I got back, that night, I had to go back home with Jamison and spend the night at his mother's house with Gerone. The next day, they helped me find an apartment on the south side of Sacramento. I moved out the few pieces of furniture that I had from my apartment and into a small one-bedroom house a block and a half down the street from Jamison mom in the South Sacramento, Franklin, area. Sometimes, I would get Jamison's sister to watch Gerone for me, and we would go on joyrides. We had become wild teenagers; we were turning into Bonnie and Clyde. We went to the colleges, and I waited with the car while the guys went and stole people's wallets out of the lockers while they were in the gym. We weren't using any birth control, and soon I discovered that I was pregnant by Jamison. We went back to a college, and they stole money again. This time we went shopping for maternity clothing because Jameson didn't have a job; he was an athlete at the high school that he attended. After I started showing more and more with the pregnancy, I wouldn't go out with them anymore. I became good friends with Jamison's sister Rena. She had a young baby about six months old already. She and I started hanging out together. We would go out to the Air Force base with Jamison's mom's friend Pam and another friend or theirs. I got a fake ID so that I could get into the clubs. We would dance and drink most of the night, getting home after 3:00 a.m. some weekends. Jamison's mom and her friend Pam enjoyed playing cards— bid whiz, and spades—and having a few drinks while playing. Soon I learned to play and joined in with Jamison and his brothers and mother. If there were too many of us playing, we would play rise and fly. I learned how to cheat at cards. It seemed as though I wasn't learning anything beneficial from this family. We would let our partner know if we had a high or low hand by talking the table, as some call it. High, we were going up town; low, we were going down town; spades, we needed to garden; hearts, we would start singing a song about heart conditions. We would stay up on the weekends until one or two o'clock drinking beer and gin and playing cards; it was right up my alley. I was never a party person unless I was drinking, so I was glad we stayed in playing cards. I had moved right down the street, and Jamison had practically moved in by now. It was only a short walk back to my house, so when he didn't want to be with me, he went back to his mom's. Tee, you know that I never talked negative about your dad to you while you were growing up. I don't want to do it know, but you asked me to tell you about the things that happened in our relationship— the reason that we didn't get married. Our relationship started to cool off. Jamison and I was constantly arguing. I decided to enroll in another high school to finish my education. When I started to show, I enrolled in a continuation school to try to finish school. Jamison would watch Gerone while I was at school. He and his fried Ollie would take him with them in his grandmother's car. One day they had gone to a store and sat him on a merry-go-round in the store by himself while they went running around in the store. Gerone was only about a year and three months old. He didn't know how to hold on, so he fell off the horse that Jamison had put him on. I had to take him to the hospital to have stitches put on the cut next to his eye. I told Jamison that he should know better than to leave my baby alone. During this pregnancy, I craved McDonald's fish sandwiches, Oreo cookies, and sweet potato pie. I don't remember craving anything when I was pregnant with Gerone, unless it was bananas or beans, which were the only thing plentiful at my dad's. I gained fifty pounds by the time my baby Tee was born. I also grew taller, which I didn't think was possible. Everyone thought that I was going to have a football player. It was a good thing that I was very active, or I would have really been a blimp. I played baseball until I was eight months pregnant and walked a lot. About a month later, Jamison had Gerone in the car and went to visit his mom and left him in the car, he said. Gerone fell out and hit his head by the time I came home from school his head was so swollen on one side that I could hardly recognize my baby. He hadn't even taken him to the doctor. When the doctor examined Gerone, he said that it looked as though someone had pushed him down some stairs the way the injury was to his head. Only God and whoever was there knows the truth. Gerone had to stay in the hospital for a week before I could bring him home. I was still determined to finish school, so I went back to school. Only a few months later, he was at the house cooking something. When we picked up the hot frying pan, he wasted hot oil on Gerone. He had sat a chair next to the stove with Gerone in it while he was cooking. I know that it was an accident, but he was too careless with my son. That was the last straw. I knew that I would have to quit school to take care of my baby. Here I was again, instead of taking care of my baby, the only one that loved me, I had left him in harm's way. Once again I had failed; this time, I failed my own child. They kept Gerone in the hospital for over two months. His skin had healed, but they wouldn't let me bring him home. I am sure that they were investigating me to see if I was abusing my child. I loved Gerone. I would never intentionally let him get hurt. Finally, after not being able to bring my baby home, I went to the hospital and stole him out. They would let me take him to the children's play area to play with the toys that they had, but I couldn't take him home. I brought his clothes with me in my purse and went into the bathroom and changed his clothes. After checking that no one was outside of the door, I took him to the elevator and out the door. I stayed away from my house all day and finally went to the house after midnight. It wasn't five minutes that I had shut the door that two policemen knocked at the door. They asked me the stupidest question: they wanted to know why I took him. I told him that he was mine and I wanted him back. After that, I stayed home with Gerone. I took him everywhere with me, not trusting Jamison to watch him any longer. I had tried to be honest with Jamison and told him about my past because I truly thought that we would get married. His mother and family would always ask us when we were getting married. His grandmother was a Christian and told us that we needed to get married especially since I was pregnant. I hadn't thought about God or church anymore since the ordeal with Raymond and him pulling the gun on me. Jamison's grandmother was like a thorn in my flesh because whenever I saw her, she would always tell me that I should come to church. She was the best part of our relationship, but I wasn't ready to go to church. I didn't understand that what I needed was a relationship with Christ. In my mind, I would just go sit in a church building and not have any fun in life. It seemed that after I told

Jamison about my past, he started going out without me a lot; we would get into altercations often. It excelled from the yelling at one another to hitting. He would shove me or push me, and I fell across the coffee table one time. Then I would get the broom and rap him across the head with it; if it wasn't the broom, then it would be the mop. It got so that I could hardly keep a broom or a mop around the house to clean. I had gone to the doctor a couple of weeks before my due date for my checkup on my pregnancy; I had been there practically all day. By the time they called me, it was a little before 5:00 p.m. I had started having pain in my back and stomach around 3:00 p.m., but they were very light. Around 4:00 p.m., I noticed that they were coming about every five minutes, but still very light. When the doctor called me in, I told him that I thought that I was going to have my baby. He checked me and told me that it was just gas. By the time I got home, the pain was much harder so, I lay down on the couch. Jamison and I had had a fight earlier that day, which had started to become commonplace with us, so he had gone to his mom's. He was staying away more often; one of his sisters told me that some girl would call his mom's house looking for him. I'm not sure what brought him back to the house that day, besides the Lord. I didn't have a phone to call him. But when he showed up, I was about to have the baby. I could feel the head trying to push out. He helped me to turn over on my back. I was screaming bloody murder, not so much that it hurt, which it did, but because I thought that I was going to die. I had just saw a movie on TV about some Indians or Eskimos—I forgot which— the night before. One of the women was pregnant and about to give birth. They took her out a little ways from the village and told her that she had to chew off the umbilical cord after the baby was born and tie it off or she would die. I thought that I was going to die because there was no way that I was chewing off a bloody umbilical card; it made me gag just thinking about it.

My landlord heard me screaming and came to see what was going on. They probably thought that Jamison and I were fighting again and it had gotten out of hand. When my landlord came back, she helped me pull off my underwear, and the baby's head crowned. At this point, Jamison took off running down to his mom's and left me there. My landlord called the ambulance for me. When the EMT got to the house, my daughter was born, and they placed her on top of my stomach and covered us both up. All the way to the hospital, I thought that I was still going to die. I was still waiting for them to cut off the umbilical cord. I couldn't figure out what they were waiting for. My baby was only five pounds and thirteen ounces. Because she was so small and I had her at home, I didn't have to have stitches, so I felt really good in the hospital. I didn't feel as though I had even had a baby. The next day, someone was playing some music and I could hear it. I got up out of the bed to go to the bathroom and started dancing around the room. I would walk around the hospital looking at the other babies instead of resting. By the evening, I had gotten an infection and was running a low-grade fever. By morning, my fever was up to a 102 degrees. When the fever went down, it would come back up the next evening. I ended up staying in the hospital for five days before they released me. Jamison's mother kept Gerone while I was in the hospital. The same day that I came home from the hospital, Jamison came to the house and wanted to take my baby down to his mom's house. Tee was born in November, and it had been raining earlier and was cold and damp outside. When I told him no, he hit me and tried to take her anyway from me. I stood my ground and refused to let him take her. She could get sick, and the way that he had taken care of Gerone—no, it was out of the question. Trina, that is what I had named her (although I call her Tee now), was just five days old, and there was no way that he was taking my baby out in the air. And Jamison sure wasn't taking my baby down there to all the germs that would be at the house with all of the people that lived there and hung out. Although I didn't have love or self-esteem for myself, I loved my children. That night, he came back and tried to get in. I had the landlord change the locks on the door, but forgot to put Jamison's clothes out with him. He put his fist through the small window next to the doorknob and opened the door. He stayed at the house for a few weeks and tried to act as though he was doing right by us. He said that he was going to take care of his baby. That was a laugh; I was the one receiving welfare, and he wasn't putting in one dime. He was constantly going out with his friends, and his sisters were telling me that he had another girlfriend. During this time, his mother had moved about a half mile away, and I would take Gerone and Trina over to visit. I was still good friends with his mother and his sisters and brothers. His sister Rena had moved into her own place when her mother moved, but she was always there visiting too. A few months after his mother moved, Rena told me that he was supposed to be going with some big overweight girl in the Heights. One night after he left, I got someone to take me to the girl's house so that I could check for myself. Sure enough, he had his grandmother's car parked outside of her house. I had a knife in my purse that I kept after the mess that I had had with the girls when I lived in the Heights. I let out all off the air in the tires and left. When Jamison came back the next day, we had a huge fight. I finally convinced him to take his clothes and get out of my house. I told him not to ever come back to my house. It wasn't like I was losing anything; he was living off my children's welfare check and mine and off of his mom and grandmother. A few days later, the girl that he was going with in the Heights and her sister sent word that she wanted to fight me. I sent back that I didn't fight over any man. I said that I didn't want him anyway, that she could have his sorry behind. I don't like mess. I am not a messy person when it comes to keeping mess going. I prefer peace, but if you push me, I will fight. The next week when I was at Jamison's mom's, his girlfriend and her sister came over saying that they wanted to fight me. To this day, I wouldn't be surprised if one of his sisters didn't call and tell them that I was there. Some of the younger ones enjoy keeping things going. It has never been my thing, but since they had come hunting me down, I was not about to go into hiding. When I went outside I had my knife in my pocket. When I walked to the car that they were in, his girlfriend's sister jumped out, talking smack and was trying to rush up on me. I grabbed her by her hair and started hitting her head into the car's hood until someone stopped me. I told her to take herself on back home and don't bother me again. I also let her know that I didn't care if she had Jamison or not. I felt that they deserved each other. Later, I heard that he had got with some lesbian, and she had beat his behind for him. What goes around comes around, what can I say?

CHAPTER

6

After my freedom from Jamison, I enjoyed my life of sin for a couple of years. I had two beautiful babies that I loved and that loved me. I found that Rita's dad and stepmother had moved back to Red Bluff with her. When I got an opportunity to talk to her, she said that she was all right. I wasn't sure because I didn't know if her stepmother was listening in on our conversation. I missed my sister. I wanted to adopt her and take her away from her parents, but I knew that if my aunts couldn't that neither could I. I didn't have any money to pay for an attorney; neither did I have money to take care of her if she could live with me. I didn't see Rita again until she had finished high school and had gotten a job at one of the local five-and-dime stores there in Red Bluff. Rena and I became close friends and started going out together after Jamison and I broke up. One of her younger sisters would babysit for us both when we went out partying with a couple of other friends. Sometimes we would go out of town to the base and party with the airmen and spend half the night with one man or another when we were bored with the clubs. I didn't have to be bothered with anyone that I didn't want to. I was just out for a good time; I didn't want anybody permanent. I was enjoying being free. When ever I needed extra spending money for my children for Christmas or something, I would look up one of the older men that I knew would give me money for a favor. I would try to imagine that they were someone else or that I was some where else, like you do when you go to the gynecologists office. There were just there to meet my needs as far as I was concerned.

I wasn't perfect, but I did the best that I knew raising my children and hardened my heart toward men because of the hurts and bad relationships I'd had. I decided that I wouldn't have any man unless he was married. All of this came from the stinking thinking of the *True Confession* magazines that I had read in my early teens. I decided that I still wanted to be a kept woman—yeah right, with two children. I hadn't tried going back to school. I was just on welfare and whatever money that I could get out of the men that I went out with. I didn't realize that it was just another step in Satan's deception to bring my life closer to the pit of hell. I dated a couple of married men after that, both at least twenty years older than I was. They would buy me groceries and give me money for my favors. I didn't care just as long as they would go home at the end of the night. I didn't have any regard for their family. I figured what they didn't know wouldn't hurt them, and it was their husbands that were no good. One of the men was a deacon in a Baptist church, and he invited me to come to his church. I wondered what that would be like: he and his wife and girlfriend sitting up in the church. I didn't know that much about church, but I knew that that wasn't right. You may be wondering what this list of men in and out of my life have to do with anything. A lot of sinners have sex with different people all of the time. What they don't know is that they are digging themselves deeper and deeper into the trap that Satan has set for them. There are also different diseases out there that you may catch and never get rid of, but by the grace of God. My best friend that I had finally made grade school in Red Bluff latter died when her husband gave her AIDS. Destroying families and taking their livelihood in not what we want to reap back for ourselves with the seeds that we sow. What I want you to see is that God, in his mercies and grace, has paid for our sins with the shed blood of His son Christ Jesus. No matter how low you have gone in life, God is there. No matter what you have done, He will save you if you ask. I know that it is hard to believe, but God loves you just as much as He loves His only begotten son Jesus. Satan will make you feel guilty after he has tricked you into doing evil, but there is no sin that God will not forgive through the shed blood of Christ. If you ask him and put your trust in Him, He is bigger than all of your sins, but there are consequences for what you do. When Gerone turned two and a half, I put him in preschool; and when Tee turned two, I put her in preschool. She was there all the time anyway, with her brother, so they let me register her. Back then, if they were potty trained, they could go to preschool. At first I usually stayed and participated with the class; later it gave me the chance to bring men to the house when my children weren't home or go meet someone at theirs. When I ran short on money, I found that there were other much older men out there that were willing to pay for a good time. Men that lied to themselves and pretended that they still had what it took to get a young woman. Men who, because of years of drinking, had robed themselves of any hope for intimacy. Sometimes, I felt as though I wanted to gag, and I hated being touched by them; but I got what I needed from them, and they got what they wanted. By my still being friends with Jamison's sister and mom, my children and I would go fishing with them and another friend of theirs, plus we still had our card games most nights. My children were most always with me when they weren't in school or unless I went out with Jamison's sister. Most of the time, Jamison wasn't there any way; he had moved in with someone else. It was none of my business as long as he left me alone. Rena and I would get together at Jamison's moms and play music when we weren't playing cards and dance to the latest tunes with her brothers. I became a good dancer. When Rena, Pam, and I went out to the clubs, I would win a pitcher of beer for our table by dancing. Guys would always ask me to dance. I made sure to leave them at the door when the party was over though. I had no wish to get into another relationship with anyone. Maybe I was finally learning some sense when it came to men, I thought. Get whatever you needed to get out in the street; just don't bring them home. I would give out fake phone numbers, fake addresses, and sometime fake names. Cal and Paul, Jamison's brothers, where my partners, and they made sure I knew all of the latest moves. I would dance so hard and let myself really get into the dance. Once when I was dancing, I felt this thing trying to take over my body. It was literally a force trying to enter into me. After that, I would watch myself when I danced and would not turn myself over to the dancing the way that I had done when I felt that spirit or force trying to evade my body. Now I know that it was an evil spirit that was trying to take over my soul and body. I say to my children, or whoever may read these pages, please do not play with Satan; he plays for keeps. People have lost their minds playing around with him; he is evil seeking whom he may devour and deceive. If you ever find yourself in a situation that you feel an evil presence near you, plead the blood of Jesus against the spirit. Just say out of your mouth, "I plead the blood of Jesus against you," or say, "The blood of Jesus cover me, in the name of Jesus." But be sure that you have asked Christ into your heart as Lord and Savior first because without Christ, you are not covered, and have no power over Satan. In the Bible, in Acts, there were men that had not received Christ as their savior and tried to cast out evil spirits in the name of the Lord Jesus, saying, "We adjure you by Jesus, whom Paul preacheth." And there were seven sons of one Sceva, a Jew and chief of the priests, which did so. And the evil spirit answered and said, "Jesus I know, and Paul I know, but who are you?" And the man in whom the evil spirit was leaped on them, and overcame them, and prevailed against them, so that they fled out of that house naked and wounded. Rena had met a guy, Olmar, that she had fallen for, and he and his cousin Nathan would come by Rena's mom's house to hang out. Rena's mom's house was a good place for hanging out and drinking a couple of beers and listening to music. Olmar's cousin was really cute, and he caught my eye. He would ask me if I wanted to go for a ride when Olmar took Rena out for a ride. He had recently moved to Sacramento from Mississippi and had an accent that I loved to hear when he talked; he also had the cutest dimples. When I learned that he was also married, it was too late; I had already fallen for him. I was once again a fool in love. Not only was he married, but also he had two children; he also drank and smoked dope. It had been several years since I had smoked any weed, but I had again picked up the bad habit of smoking cigarettes. It was like someone had put some kind of root or mojo on me. I had to have him at any cost. I would drive his car and pass by his house, hoping that his wife saw me in it. I wanted to break them up so that I could have him. I would call her and tell her that I wanted her husband and I wanted her kids too. I had never had anything like this happen to me before. I had even told Rena that I was going to get someone to put a fix on him so that he couldn't leave me. I had gone so far as to get some of his hair and was trying to get a piece of his clothing. I tell you that Satan had a hook in me concerning that man. I tell you that that is some scary stuff to want someone like that. The only reason that I didn't get someone to put a fix on him is because Rena and her mom told me that if I did that, I may want to get tired of him one day and couldn't. After that, I decided to leave well enough alone. I had heard of people being fixed by someone and they couldn't get rid of the person until they killed them when they tried to leave them. I wasn't superstitious, but I was fearful. Rena told me that Nathan's wife was saved. I didn't understand what *saved* really meant at that time; all I knew was that I wanted her husband. I am sure that she was saved now because no one would have put up with my mess. I believe that she was praying for me even then. One day a few months later, Nathan was driving by as I was on my way to Rena's mom's; he told me to get into the car. I don't know what happened but just as I was going to say something to him and get into the car, out of my mouth came, "You better go home to your wife." He was shocked; I was flabbergast. I didn't want him to go home. I wanted him to be with me. I couldn't believe that I had told him that. As I stood there staring at him, something happened in me. He didn't look so good to me anymore; the excitement that I felt when I saw him left me. Then I repeated my words: "You better go home to your wife." Without another word, he drove off. After he drove off, I wondered why I had said that. Now I know that God had a different plan for my life. After I had sent Nathan back to his wife, whether he went or not wasn't my problem. I met his cousin—another Nathan. I think they were both named after a grandfather or something. I was so tired of my crazy life, by this time, I was looking for a serious change. This Nathan went to church. By my not being associated with anyone that went to church other than my dad that went to a Seventh Day Adventist church, that didn't count with me. You see, when we went to church with him, we went straight back out of the door while he wasn't looking when we were supposed to be going to Sabbath school. The offering that my dad gave us made good spending money at the little store around the corner from his church. The only other person was Dear Dallings, Jamison's grandmother. Dear was really my only example of a Christian person that I believed lived what she said. Since she went to a different kind of church, I thought that that must be the best kind to go to, if you were going to go at all. I just wasn't ready yet. I kept on living what I thought was a good life. There was a time that I also turned my back on God. I didn't want to hear His name, and I didn't want to talk to anyone that went to the so-called church. And please don't tell me that Jesus loves me because I knew that he couldn't love me because of what he allowed to happen in my life. Nathan Dennis invited me to go to church with him. Wooh, how lucky could I get. He was handsome, well built, but just a little short for me; but when he wore his boots, which he did all of the time, we were the same height. About once a month, he would take me to this little Hispanic church. He took me to meet his family, and I became friends with them. I believed that he was a true Christian. What he hadn't counted on was my actually getting saved. We would make love whenever he came over, and I was happy again. I found out that happiness does not last. Inner joy from God is what will carry you through if you ask for it. I had changed my lifestyle since I had met Nathan Dennis. I didn't go out partying anymore. God took the desire to smoke cigarettes from me right after I had broken up with his cousin. I had also stopped drinking. One night, a New Year's Eve night to be exact. I was lonely and wanted to do something. Since Nathan hadn't come over, I decided to go to this little church not too far from me. They were having a revival with a young black minister. I had enjoyed the singing, and when they had an altar call, I found myself at the front of the church with some other people that had gone up to receive Christ. I hadn't meant to go forward; in fact, I still don't know how I got there unless I was transported up front. But when they asked us if we wanted to be saved, I suppose I said yes. The next thing I know, I was getting up off the floor; no one had put their hand on me. Actually, no one was even paying attention to me when I looked around. I didn't know what happened, but I do know that I had been changed on the inside. I became hungry for God's word and started reading it every day and praying. I started going to church more often. One day, I came across the word *fornicate* in the Bible and I asked Nathan what it meant. He told me that it wasn't for us, but I still wanted to know what it meant. Nathan told me to ask the minister at the church. So the next time I went back to the little Hispanic church, I asked the minister what the word meant. He wouldn't tell me, but he gave me a Bible that had a dictionary in the back, so I looked it up. When I saw that it meant having sex without being married, I told Nathan that we were not supposed to be having sex. Again, he told me that it wasn't for us. Because he had been in the church much longer than I had been, I thought that he knew more about it. As I continued to read the Bible, the word kept coming up. God had begun to deal with me about it, and I was feeling more and more convicted whenever we had sex. When I finally refused to have sex anymore with Nathan, he forced himself on me. That was the last time that we had sex then. When I realized that I had missed my monthly cycle, I knew that I was pregnant. I continued going to church and praying more and more. God knew that I would need His strength in the time to come. When Nathan finally did come over after a couple of months, I told him that I was pregnant. He told me that I had better pray that I wasn't because he had gone back to his wife. I didn't even know that he had a wife to go back to. He was just another man out to get what he could. Needless to say, I was devastated. I couldn't believe that someone that said they were saved could do that to me. Of course I blamed God. I felt that He had messed up my life too many times. Here I was, twenty years of age, pregnant with my third child, and confused as ever.

After crying until there were no more tears, I quit going to church. I denied in my mind that I was pregnant, and my body went along, believing that I was not pregnant. My monthly cycle returned, and all of the symptoms that were associated with pregnancy disappeared. I did not want to associate with anyone that went to church or even hear the word *God*. My Bible sat where I last placed it, collecting dust, because I didn't want to touch it. Some people have lost faith in God or are holding on with the last ridges of the tips of their fingernails. I was one of them; there was a time in my life that I would have cut off my own fingernails purposely to let go of God. I am glad that He did not let go of me. I know that you have asked the question, "How can God who is supposed to be so good and loving let this happen to me or to someone that we love?" Why do bad things happen to good people? There is none good but God, but some people that we have esteemed as good people do make bad choices. I have made plenty in my life. When disasters happen, you can believe that God has been trying to speak to us or get our attention before it happens. God is always trying to get us to make right decisions and direct us into choosing life. Satan is the prince of death; he comes to steal, kill, and destroy. But God does allow some evil things to happen when we don't listen to that small voice in our conscious. When we look around and see disasters happen, we want to know why God allowed it to happen, for instance, tsunamis, earthquakes that kill thousands or the 9/11 disaster. God can use disasters to get us to reflect on Him although He is not the cause of the disasters. God has many ministering angels or spirits helping us every day that we aren't aware of. Most of the time we are unaware of their help because the thing that Satan planned for you did not happen. The car didn't hit you this time. When there are so many people killed at once, it gets our attention; but at some point in time, those same people would have died anyway sooner or later. One or two deaths at a time does not get our attention like several at one time does. God can use this to speak to our hearts although He did not cause the deaths. Wherever you are and whatever you are doing in your life, God is there. He is a Spirit, always present, ready, and willing to show His unlimited love and favor to us. Sometimes we are so filled with the cares of this present world that we can't even imagine that He is right there with us, whispering to us, beckoning to us to come to Him so that He can help us. All we can see is the things that are wrong, or what we want, not how He may have directed us to miss a disaster. And even in the disasters that happen around us, He's trying to get our attention to stop going in the direction we are going. It is the goodness of God that works repentance, but some people will not heed His goodness. It takes more to get their attention. Most of the time, life is too loud to hear Him if you don't take the time to stop and listen. He (God) also gave us another gift besides his Son Christ Jesus; He gave us the Holy Spirit to help us. When we see ourselves as God sees us—as cherished, and loved children, and we see Him as Father or (Abba or Daddy)—it will be easier for us to see others in love too. We couldn't pay for our sins, and neither can they. It is God's undeserved favor and grace that saves us through Jesus Christ, and not we ourselves. As we grow in the word, it will become easier to forgive because we know that we didn't do anything to deserve to be forgiven. There was no amount of money that we could have paid for salvation. Jesus paid it all. We are not saved by our good works but by believing on what Jesus did for us on the cross and knowing that He is willing to help us if we ask; it does get easier I had started back partying and going out. I went back to smoking, drinking—just living my life the way I wanted to. About six months later, God, in His infinite mercies, met me one day in my living room. No, I did not see God. But He met me nevertheless. It was one of my rare days that I wasn't at the preschool with my children. I was walking through the house and had walked into the living room still with hatred in my heart for any Christian or church goers. When God spoke to me, I don't know if it was in my head or if it was in the room with me; there is no way I could tell you, but He spoke to me just as if someone had walked into the room and started talking to me. It was as though we just picked up in the middle of a conversation that we were having. God said that everybody is not like that, and I knew instantly what the conversation was about. At first I didn't know that it was God; when I looked around I didn't see anyone. So I said, "What?" He repeated, "Everybody is not like that." I don't know how I knew what He was talking about, but I knew that He was referring to Nathan and his hypocrisy; and I answered in a voice full of pent-up emotion through gritted teeth, "Yes, they are." I wasn't just speaking about Nathan; I was speaking about every man that I had ever known and been hurt by, including my dad. He didn't argue with me but continued with the conversation, in a voice so full of love. "If you want to live right, you can." And that was the end of the conversation. I stood there analyzing the words that he left me with. Could I really? I wanted to ask questions, I wanted to talk to Him longer. How did He know what I was thinking? But then He is God. I wasn't so sure that I could live a Christian lifestyle, but I was willing to try. At that time, I did not understand that it was believing right that would cause me to live right, believing that it was Jesus's righteousness not mine that would make me righteous. But God knew. I was afraid that I would fail and be a hypocrite and end up causing someone to not turn to Christ if I messed up. I would have rather not said that I was living for Christ than to cause someone to turn his or her back on God as I had. I promised myself that if I ever backslid, I would tell people that I was no longer living for God so that they wouldn't look at my life and say that God was a lie. What I found was that apart from Christ, I could do nothing; and I did end up walking away from God again, accusing God for not providing for me because I didn't have the patience to wait for his direction and guidance for my life. I began attending another church and started going for noon prayer and Sunday service. I read my Bible and prayed at home. Some of the ladies met at the lunch hour to pray, and one of these was Dot. She was a very sweet person, and we talked several times. She invited me home with her to meet her parents whom she still lived with at age eighteen. Dot also had one child. One day our conversation turned to guys and she mentioned Nathan's name. When I asked what his last name was, I found that we had been dating the same person at the same time. I was just the one that ended up pregnant by him. He had even taken her to meet his family. How foolish I felt to have believed that he cared for me. By the time that the revelation concerning Nathan came, she had already broken off with dating him. Some of the women in Nathan's family gave me some clothes that they felt were appropriate for church. I didn't have any dresses only pants, and this church was very religious and dominating. Most of the young adults wore long skirts and dresses. The more mature women wore suits. Because Nathan's aunts and sister were several years older than I was, they gave me some suits to wear, but almost as soon as I made the decision to live for God, He let me know that I was indeed pregnant. The realization that I was pregnant came flooding back along with all of the symptoms. It seemed as if I started showing overnight; whereas I had lost twenty pounds in the last six months, now I began to gain some of the weight back. I say it was the shortest pregnancy that I ever had. For me, it only lasted about three months longer once I allowed myself to acknowledge the pregnancy. When I started showing, I was so embarrassed when I walked into church, but my pride wouldn't let me hang my head. It was not that I didn't want my baby; it was the stares and whispers that I got, some imagined and some not. It wasn't that anyone was ever anything but caring toward me, but I knew that they were saying things about me. I was also alone and didn't know what I would do when it came the time for me to deliver. What would happen to my children when I went into the hospital? I had so much fear of circumstances, and I was still hurting about what had transpired between Nathan and myself. I was still full of anger and was untrusting. After Nathan and I had broken up, I met and went out with an older man, thinking that he wouldn't be as immature as the younger ones that I had been dating. One day coming from Rena's mom's house, this cute guy drove up and offered me a ride. I refused his offer. A few months later, as I was walking home again, he drove up again and offered me a ride; this time I accepted. He seemed nice enough, and this was the days before so many people started disappearing. He treated me good, giving me money to help buy groceries for the children, and buying me gifts. But I could never really trust him; in my heart I knew if he dated me and he had told me that he was married, I felt that he would do the same to me if we got together. I was still pregnant, so we just became friends at that time. I would walk a great deal of the time, about half mile each way almost every day, pushing Tee in a stroller and letting Gerone stand on the back of the stroller as I pushed them or walk beside it if I wasn't going very far. John would visit a couple of times a month. I didn't have to be bothered with him every day. In talking with him, I found out that he was a deacon in the church that he attended and that he was married, which was fine by me. I still had a lot of hatred in me. Because I received Christ in my life, I still had a lot of growing to do. When it got close to the time for me to have my baby, one of Nathan's aunts at the church said that my children and I could come stay at her house until I had the baby. She was a very sweet lady and she loved God; she and her husband were separated, and it was just her and her children living with her. She gave me a room that the three of us shared. A couple of days after we went to stay with her, I woke up one night in labor. I didn't know it at the time, but God had provided for me again. When the nurses brought my baby to me in the hospital, he was so white and bald. I didn't understand that the children could go back a generation and take their grandparents' genes. My other babies were little tan babies with thin slick hair when they were born; this one was whiter than the little white babies that I saw when I went to the nursery. I was confused. I knew that I hadn't been with anyone else except Nathan, who was a light-brown complexion and brown eyes. My baby had blue eyes when he opened them. When I went home and Nathan came over to see him, I was waiting to go through the same thing with him as I had with Gerone's dad. But to my amazement Nathan said that he looked just like his father, who I didn't know was white, and Drew had taken after his grandfather. It didn't matter though because we were not getting back together. After Drew was born, John asked me out several times, and we started having sex; he had told me that he was married, but I didn't care. I didn't feel that I could trust any other kind. He went to his church, and I went to mine. I was still growing; I didn't grow up in church, so God had a lot of work to do on me. Although I said that I would live for God, I didn't know what it really was about. I figured if I didn't lie to people, fornicate too often, or deceive them as they had me, I was fine. We dated several months until I got tired of him. He was just too short for my taste. I didn't like going out with him because he was so short. I would walk about three or four feet behind him or as far to the side as I could get. I didn't care if his feelings was hurt. I didn't really care about him. I know that I didn't respect him because he was a hypocrite just like Nathan. I didn't believe that there were any good men at all; they were all liars and cheats. A few months after John and I broke up I met Don; he was tall about six foot two. We started dating after I had determined that he also was married. We dated on and off for a couple of years. My dad bought me a little car to get around after I had Drew; that really helped me. I didn't know much about cars other than putting gas in them and driving where I wanted to go. Needless to say, it didn't last long without checking the oil and other things that needed to be done. There were times that Rena and I wanted to go out that I actually stole gas to go out of town or to the Air Force base to party, looking for excitement. I didn't know that I was hungry for a relationship with God. I always thought that I was a good person, but when I go over my past life, I see that I need Jesus in my life. In the church that I had been attending, the pastor was so strict that you could barely do anything but pray, breathe, and eat. I would go to church with my heart ready to receive the word of God and got beat down with the condemnation preaching so bad that I left feeling worse than I did when I went. I never felt that I was good enough. I always saw God waiting to point a finger at me or send me to hell if I stepped to the right or left. I had not been taught that we are saved by God's grace and made in the righteousness of God by His Son Christ Jesus. I didn't know that we are not saved by works but by faith in the shed blood of Christ and what he suffered through on the cross for us to have. Most of the people that I knew in the church were so self-righteous. We were taught that we had to work to be saved, keep every commandment perfectly when no one could, except Christ. I was the subject of the Sunday message several times. The pastor told the young women not to be associated with me because I told them that they should wear pants when they were gardening. The pastor was against women wearing pants. Most all the women wore long skirts, but long skirts don't hide sin. I had slowly stopped going to church and had started going back out. It was what is known as backsliding. I never even told Don that I went to church. Both John and Don were much older than I was; they were both in their forties, and I was in my early twenties. I knew that I didn't have to be bothered with them if I didn't want to because they were both married. Don got crazy and started saying that he was going to get a divorce from his wife and marry me. I didn't think so; I figured that he would just do me the same way that he did his wife, so I had to kick him to the curb as well. I enjoyed being the kept woman; they would give me money and buy me gifts. This was what I had desired in my teenage years, and it was somehow still in the back of my mind as an achievement. I just needed men with more money than these had. When Drew was a few months old, I needed to find a bigger place since there were four of us now. So I started my house hunt. I soon found a bigger place. What I didn't know was that I was moving next door to a prayer warrior, who was praying for me. I soon found out that there wasn't enough good in me to keep me out of trouble. I needed to learn how to cast my cares to God because he cared for me instead of me trying to keep myself. Besides Satan, will make sure that you fail when you don't have the understanding of God's word and wisdom. I had—and have—a lot of growth ahead of me still. Whenever my children's dads came over, I would find myself in bed with one or the other. Two of them are married now, and I hadn't seen Gerone's dad in a few years. The other two had no problem with committing adultery, but when it was over, I would be the one guilty and ashamed and condemned that I had yet again failed. I knew that I didn't mean anything to them since they were both married to someone else and not me. I don't even believe that they were coming to see their kids. Who would want me? I guess I was just what people considered a quick lay, just trash. But thank God that he had another plan for my life. I was lonely and I did what I did to have somebody, but it wasn't the right somebody. After a few years of this on-and-off relationships with them, I began seeing Nathan again, not my baby's daddy but his cousin that was married. The one I thought I couldn't do without. God had blessed me to move into a nice apartment when I was going to church and to buy my first new car. I had plenty of clothes and a good job. I had gotten my GED and started college, and I was buying a house on my own, had just signed the papers. All I needed to do was pick up the key on closing. It wasn't enough for me. I became disillusioned because I wanted a husband. A lot of the young women at the church were getting married, and I was feeling left out. I felt that if God would give me a husband, I wouldn't have the need to be with these guys. So again I turned my back on God. I began smoking drugs with Nathan and drinking again. The ways of a transgressor is hard. The first thing that went sour was that I lost my job and I lost my clothes. I had taken my good clothes off the hangers in the closet and put them in the bottom of my closet to take to the cleaners. The toilet somehow over flowed and the water ran into the closet under the wall without my knowing it and ruined my clothes. I lost my house that I hadn't moved into yet—and my children's respect. I made sure that everybody that knew that I was saved now knew that I had backslid. Although I was mad with God, I wasn't going to be a hypocrite and cause someone to lose his or her soul because of me. I would tell my friends that I had backslid all of the time, especially if I was drinking. I felt so guilty. I was always talking about God but made sure they knew I wasn't living for Him. They didn't want to be around me because I kept talking about God, reminding them that they needed to be saved. I was now no good to the world and no good to the church or myself. One day, Nathan came over with some weed for us to smoke before we had sex. My two oldest children were at school and Drew was taking his nap. He wouldn't show up mostly until he thought that my children were asleep or at school and the baby was down for his nap. I know that it wasn't me that he really wanted, but I was lonely for a man's company. We sat on the couch and smoked the joint. I didn't know that it had angel dust in it. As though the joint wasn't enough, I left him there and walked across the street and got some malt beer to add to my trouble. On my way to the 7-Eleven store, which was only about one hundred fifty feet from the door of my apartment, I started hallucinating. When I attempted to step off the curb, it seemed to be about twenty-five feet down. I had to reason in my mind that I knew that it was only about four inches as I clumsily stepped down. I got the beer and headed back home. It took me a few minutes to get back up the sidewalk and get to my door. While we were sitting on my couch smoking and drinking, I began hallucinating again. I could see myself through the wall of my apartment. I could see outside without looking through a window. I could see myself floating across the grass of the apartment outside. In the hallucination,

I saw myself coming into the apartment and going into the kitchen and get a butcher knife out of the drawer. As I was watching myself, an evil force prompted me to go into the kitchen and get a knife and kill myself. When I told Nathan what was happening to me, he wanted to leave. I let him know in no uncertain terms that he was not leaving me in this condition. I was so scared; all I could see was myself committing suicide and going to hell.

I heard this small voice inside of me telling me to plead the blood of Jesus. I reasoned in my head that there was no way that I could do that—after all, look what I was doing? God wouldn't hear me. I had turned my back on Him for a man, someone else's husband— one that would leave me and let me kill myself. Was this what I gave God up for? Again, I heard the small voice telling me to plead the blood of Jesus. Very quietly, I said, "The blood of Jesus." It just barely came out of my lips, but I could feel the evil force diminishing a little. When I stopped pleading the blood of Jesus, it came back. I began to plead the blood of Jesus a little louder; as I felt the force backing off, I became bolder with the words. Nathan heard me and really got scared and wanted to leave, but I told him he would not leave me until that stuff had worn off. After an hour or so, I could feel that the spirit had left me. Nathan made no pretenses about trying to get out of there. God is merciful in His love. The next week, Nathan came by again—I suppose to see if I was still alive or not. And again, we sat and smoked weed with angel dust in it. I figured that if I didn't drink the beer and malt liquor with it, I would be all right. I didn't hallucinate this time, but I could feel that suicide spirit coming back. I couldn't believe that I had been fool enough to try it again. I again pleaded the blood of Jesus over myself, this time promising myself that I wouldn't do it again. I know that Satan wanted me out of the way, maybe even to prevent this book from being written so that someone would be helped. After that ordeal, Nathan and I went our separate ways.

CHAPTER 7

After breaking off with Nathan and almost committing suicide, I went back to church. My friend Dot's mom and dad, Essie and Will, took me into their family. I got off of welfare and found a job and started working. God had once again began blessing my life. Shortly after I had my son Drew, Dot's mom and dad and their entire family adopted my children and me into their family. Although I was twenty- one by then, they typed up papers and had a big celebration and party to invite us into their family; for once, I felt like I belonged. My new adopted godmother, whom I know God blessed me with, became the mother that I had lost as a child. God will restore to you what the enemy has stolen and what the cankerworm has eaten from our lives. While still trying to live saved by my own strength, I would occasionally fall into sin when Drew's dad came over, pretending he wanted to see Drew. By now, Drew was in preschool, and his Dad knew that he wasn't at home. I would pray and ask God to take Nathan out of my heart, to help me to refuse him. I knew that he didn't care for me; he just used me the way every other man had done. He would say hurtful things to me, but I would find myself in bed with him anyway. This went on off and on for a couple of years until one day, I found myself pregnant again by Nathan. I didn't use birth control because it was not my intentions to have sex. I truly wanted to live for the Lord, but I didn't have the strength to say no. I was devastated again. What would people say about me? I was in church, and now I was pregnant. I knew that no one would surely want me with three children let alone four. Finally, after a few weeks of tormenting myself with what people would think of me, I went to my pastor's wife and secretly told her what had happened. She looked me in my eyes and told me to get an abortion. I was shocked but relieved; it was a way out. She was a very humble, kind, and sweet woman. I would have never expected this to come out of her mouth. It made me wonder how many others had come to her pregnant and was told to get an abortion. I didn't think that she would confide in her husband, the pastor, about this, so I made the decision to go ahead with the procedure. I also wondered, because her husband did not believe in birth control, if she had ever gotten one, they had quite a few children of their own. The day before the procedure, I had to go get something implanted inside of me that was supposed to start the abortion. The relief turned to fear and loathing for myself. How could I do this to my baby? I would do it because of my pride and wanting to appear as righteous because of all of the self-righteous people that attended that church. My children and I spent the night at the pastor's and his wife's house so that I could go to the doctor early the next morning. It wasn't unusual that people stayed over at their home so I didn't think that it looked to be out of the ordinary. I tried not to let myself think about what I was doing, but I did afterward. I had nightmares for years of myself walking down the street and little babies dropping out of me. They were so small and weak that some were dying on the sidewalk. I prayed for God's forgiveness over and over, but I couldn't forgive myself. Until years later when I heard a message on an audio tape that a woman wrote, of how God uses Cracked Pots; I seemed to have not only cracks but holes in my salvation. The book told of how God is a forgiving God and his mercy endures forever. He loved me, but I still didn't know it at this time in my life. I thought that he was sitting in heaven, waiting for me to make another mistake, which so many of his people think because we don't understand that we have been forgiven of past, present, and future sins when we receive Christ's atonement for our sins. I don't care what the abortionist tell you about the baby just being a fetus. Satan will make sure that you live in condemnation and guilt for killing an innocent life even though they are not developed in the early months; they are just more than a blob of tissue. I can tell you because I saw what the one looked like when I had the miscarriage in my early teens. It had hands and arms; it had legs and a head. The head was large because the brain was developing, and I believe that they have feelings. I could see the imprint of the eyes that were forming on the face. God's word said, "I knew you before I formed you in your mother's womb." I sometimes weep at the loss of my babies, but I believe that I will see them again in heaven. Some believe that we will even raise them. I don't know if it is true or not, but if it is, I will know how to show and teach them love by then. You may feel that you have a right to do with your body as you wish, but that fetuses is someone else separate from you. God is using your body to sustain them but they belong to Him. So many of us have made wrong choices trying to take our own life in our hands, believing that we don't need God in our lives. If you have ever made a mistake, made a wrong choice in life, or wonder how you got into the messes that you find yourself in, trust your life to God; let Him fix it. I am writing to those that have been hurt in life and need healing. It is for those that have been through more than a sore throat or those who bumped their funny bone into a door jamb in passing. As Jesus told the accusers of the woman that was caught in adultery, he that has no sin cast the first stone. If you have never gone through anything, it is hard to be compassionate to anyone else. Jesus did not come to earth as judge; He came to show us the grace of God and His love for us. One day, He will return as Judge; but for now, He is giving us a chance to come to the Father God through Him. God knows that without his grace, we cannot live a life pleasing to Him. When we ask Jesus Christ to be Lord and savior of our lives, God makes us His righteousness. Jesus gives us His righteousness in exchange for our sin. When God sees us, He sees us through Jesus; He doesn't see us as sinners. Satan has set out to destroy the people's lives that he uses to destroy our lives by causing us to be so guilty that we think that God doesn't want us. Although many things happen to us without our permission, the enemy of our souls also deceives us into making wrong choices in our lives and making us believe that we have the right to retaliate, belittle someone, or get revenge. Without the wisdom of God and His word, it is easy to fall into his trappings. He hates God so much that he does not care whom he uses; Satan will use you to destroy someone and then turn around and destroy you. When I gave God my life, God gave me beauty for my trash heap. He will do the same for you.

The abortion turned out to be my deliverance from Nathan, my youngest son's dad. He told me to get the abortion because he didn't want any more children. I found that he already had several by several different women. I told him that when the baby left my body, that anything that I ever felt for him would also go with it. A couple of months after I had the abortion, he came back to my apartment when the children were at school and tried to have sex with me. When I told him to get out of my house and never come back, he tried to force me to have sex with him. I grabbed his arm and bit it as hard as I could. He was running around my living room hollering with me hanging on to him. It seemed that I had turned into a pit bull because I hung on to that arm and wouldn't let it go. I tried to pull a plug out of his arm. When I finally let it go, he looked at me and told me that I was crazy. I calmly reminded him of what I had said when the baby left my body—that anything that I ever felt for him would leave too, and it did. I can't begin to tell you the freedom that I felt that day from him. To not be a servant to something that you have longed to be free of is awesome. He gives you beauty for ashes time after time. I can identify in the Bible in the book of Luke, about the woman in the city that was a sinner whom God delivered from a life of sin, bought an alabaster box; and she knelt at his feet behind him, weeping, and began to wash his feet with tears and wipe them with the hairs of her head and kissed his feet and anointed them with ointment. I continued in church, more or less existing, not living and not enjoying my life at all. More couples got married and had families. I had my children and I loved them, but I didn't know how to show my love for them other than making sure that they were fed and clean. I had no one to show me how to raise children, no experience. I wasn't quite on board with some of the ways my godfather handled his sons. My dad had been overly strict, and it had not been good for me. What I saw and learned from the people that I went to church with was that children should be seen and not heard. I didn't think that anyone wanted me with three children, so I began to lose hope. The only enjoyment that I had was when I would visit my godmother. Most of the time we would buy food and snacks or eat out when we went shopping. It seemed that that was all the majority of the Christian people did for fun. Most were not healthy, didn't eat healthy food or exercise. I also enjoyed when we would take the children and all go on fishing or on a camping trip. They would always laugh at me because I would wear my earrings and dress up to go fishing. They knew that I was secretly looking for a husband. On occasion, we would go on a vacation together with the whole family, driving two or three cars caravanning. This was the first time that I had even heard that people went on vacations. At the church that we attended at the time we were always taught to put most all of our money in church. Once I had even put my bill money in church and my lights were turned off. When we don't read the word of God for ourselves, we can be led wrong. The Bible tells us to owe no one anything but to give them love. You should always pay your bills. If God ever asks you to give all your money, he will tell you; no one else will need to tell you. And if God does so, He will provide for you what is needed. Don't be deceived. When Gerone was about eight, his dad had ran into my sister Patsy at the restaurant that she and her husband (that she married after she graduated from high school) had bought. Allen had asked about Gerone and me. She had given him my phone number so that he could get in touch with me. She let me know that she had seen him and given him my number just in case he called. After about a month, Allen called and asked if he could see Gerone. I had seen some of his family members on occasion, and they always commented on how much he looked like Allen. I suppose that they had passed on to him how much Gerone looked like him. I gave him permission to come by the apartment with the understanding that if he didn't believe that Gerone was his son, that he would never let on to him who he was. Gerone had not yet asked me about who his dad was, and I wasn't sure of what I would tell him when that time came. On Allen's arrival I introduced him to Gerone as someone that I knew earlier in my life. I knew that Allen saw himself in Gerone immediately because of his funny little grin that I recognized from the past when he felt as though he was one up on you, like when he found out that I had been raped at school. If he had looked in the mirror, he would have seen himself as a young child. They looked so much alike. Allen asked if they could go outside and talk. After talking for about forty minutes, they came back in; Allen was smiling, but Gerone looked disinterested. When Allen left, I was left to explain why he had not been in his life. I did the best that I could without making his dad out to be a criminal. I didn't want to talk down about his dad. I decided that I would let him find out what type of person Allen was for himself. Gerone hasn't forgiven his dad for his abandonment, but I pray that he will one day soon. At this time in my life, I was working as a cook. A friend of mine had put in a good word for me at the convalescent hospital, and they had hired me. I had to catch a bus with my children from the south part of Sacramento to Oak Park to drop them off at my godmother's, which was about ten miles from my apartment. Then, I would catch another bus out to Sacramento State College, which was the last stop for the bus. I would then walk another mile to get to work. It was hard, but I was determined to stay off welfare. One day, I had dropped my children off and was at the bus stop when one of the older guys that I use to date, Don, stopped and asked me if I wanted a ride. Hating the long walk from the college, I accepted. I started seeing him outside of church. I was just past my midtwenties, and he was in his fifties now. I really didn't think anyone younger would want to be bothered with anyone with so many children. By now, he and his wife were divorced. Go figure. We would take rides that included the children, and he began to give me gifts again. Eventually, he asked me to marry him. I said that I needed to think about it for a while. My children were happier now that they stayed with my godmother when I was at work. Essie was the only grandmother-type of person that my children had known. I believed that she loved them and they loved her. I felt that

God had given me the mother that I needed in this part of my life. I could talk to her about most anything, and she would tell me about her feelings as well. I introduced her to Don. I wanted to get her view on him because I had made so many mistakes with men that I didn't want to make another one. Of course he put his charm on to win her over. She said that he seemed nice, just a bit old for me. I was glad that I finally had someone to help me with advice about men. Essie and I had a good relationship; I think that we spent more time talking and sharing than she did with her own children at times. We would go out to lunch and shop together, something that I desire to do with my daughter. Because of my past life, my older children hold some things against me, but God is faithful. He will give us the desires of our hearts if our ways please him. Our relationships are growing stronger each year. Don would take me to work or met me at the bus stop and pick me up and take me home so that the children didn't have to stay there all night when I got off late. My children seemed to like him enough, but I wasn't sure that I wanted someone that old. I really don't think they cared one way or another; they were just glad to be going places they hadn't seen before. He was closer to my godparent's age, and I found out that he didn't even have his own teeth now. I was looking for work that was nearer to where I lived so that I didn't need to keep walking and taking my children on the bus. On weekends, it was even harder to get to work, but I went. After working for three months, I was able to buy myself a car. My godfather had found one that was a good deal, so I bought it. It was a stick shift, and I didn't know how to drive it. I was thankful that Will took the time to show me how to drive the car. Years ago, my dad had taught me how to drive an old stick shift truck, but I had forgotten how to use the clutch. I had gotten pretty good at driving my car around town because there were no real hills to come to a rest at a stop sign in Red Bluff. One day, Pop (that is what I had started to call Will) made plans to go on a family fishing outing. I decided to follow in my car. Once we found a spot that we were going to stop at, we were going to turn the cars around so that they would be headed out. We needed to turn around on the levee road before we parked. When I tried to make a

U-turn, I had to go off the road slightly down the levee to turn around. I could not figure out how to use the clutch to keep it from rolling down the hill. I had to keep one foot on the break and the clutch while Pop came around and got in on the passenger side of the car to help me. If he hadn't been there, my car would have gone into the water. A few months later, when I thought that I could drive it well enough, my godmother and I decided that we would go to San Francisco. This time I had to park on a steep hill. I had a work out in Frisco between having to come to a stop at the stop signs on hills and parking, but I made it without rolling down the hill while I tried to remember the driving booklet from the DMV. Christmas was coming up, and I wanted to take the day off work because I had never been away from my children on Christmas before. But because I was the new person, they scheduled me to work on Christmas Day. So I quit my job after I got my paycheck just a few days before Christmas. I went shopping and got our first real live tree. We had fun decorating it together. Since I had had a decent-paying job, I was able to get the kids some nice things for once. I knew that I needed to get another job right away so that I would be able to pay my rent and buy food for the following month, but we enjoyed that Christmas.

One evening, my god sister Dot asked me if I would ride with her to church because her husband was out of town and she had invited a young man to come with her. We were still attending the self-righteous church that I had been going to, and she knew not to ride with another man alone in her car or suffer being talked about. It was dark when she picked me up, so the guy really didn't get a good look at me when Dot introduced him to me as Lou. I didn't see him again until the following week. After picking me up she then stopped and picked up the man that she had invited. She introduced him to me. I could smell that he had been smoking marijuana earlier; the scent was in his clothes. I really wasn't interested in him. I was just coming along for the company. My children were happy to stay at my godmother's until we returned.

At church, it was just another message on going to hell, so I wasn't impressed with anything that went on that night. I was still job hunting and was driving down the street a week later when the Holy Spirit inspired me to go into the convalescent hospital that I was just about to pass by. When I went in and applied for the cooking position that was open, I was hired immediately, even without a background check. My supervisor took me to the kitchen to introduce me to the staff, and who was there but Lou, the guy my god sister had introduced me to. She began introducing me to the ladies first, but when she got to Lou, I interrupted her saying that I already knew his name. He was amazed at my words and declared that I didn't know him. When I smiled and said that his name was Lou, his mouth fell open, and everyone else in the dietary department started laughing. He didn't remember me at all. I had to remind him that I was the one that rode with him and my god-sister to church the week before.

After I had worked at my new job for a few weeks, Lou started asking me to invite him over for dinner. That wasn't about to happen; first of all, I wasn't used to feeding men unless they were supplying the groceries. I was enjoying my new cooking position as second cook and wasn't about to mess it up with some guy on the job; besides that, it was only a few minutes from my apartment. I could run home on my lunch break and check on my children. After the first couple of weeks, I decided to let them stay home to save on babysitting money. My oldest was twelve, just lawful to not need a babysitter. Since my shift didn't start until 10:00 a.m., I could get them off to school, go home to check on them when they got home from school, and get back to work. I trained them to never answer the door to anyone, not even me. Everything was coming together for me. Now that I had my own car, I didn't need Don to drop me off any longer, so he just came over at night or on the weekend. Having my own car, I was no longer stranded or needing to wait on someone to give me a ride. I needed to go to one of the retail stores in the area. While I was shopping, I spotted Don at a distance. I started to walk in his direction and stopped when I saw that he was with someone. About that time, he looked up and saw me; he actually tried to hide. When he saw that I had spotted his female friend, he left her standing there and came over to me grinning. When I asked who his friend was, he went back to her with me following and introduced me as a friend that he knew. I looked at him as though he had two heads and walked off. That was the last time that I saw him. He called once trying to explain, but it was no use. I had been played by others, but to have this old goat trying to play me was too much. I fixed my attention on my job and family. I was through with men. At first, I wouldn't give Lou the time of day. I knew that he smoked weed because he would go out for lunch and come back with his eyes red and smelling of weed. Lou was always in the company of either the women or some of his male friends on his breaks. I wasn't interested in that type of man again. I didn't need a player. I had finally gotten my life into a more normal routine with the kids and my job, and I was no longer shopping for a man. Once in a while, I would catch Lou watching me, but I ignored him. After a few months, he started to tease me and asked me to invite him over for a spaghetti dinner. I had no problem telling him no. There were a couple of older ladies that worked in the kitchen, one that was saved that I had respect for. Lou asked them to ask me to invite him over for a spaghetti dinner, but I still refused to.

After his continuous teasing and getting the ladies to talk to me, I finally gave in and invited him over. I didn't know why I should invite him over; I felt that he should have asked me out instead. Later, I found out that he wanted to know if I could cook before he committed himself. When Lou came over, he brought a Marie Callender's apple pie with him. I think that was what got my attention; if he had brought flowers or some other gift, I don't think that it would have interested me as much. He said that he brought the pie so that everybody could have some of it. After my children went to bed, we sat and talked for a while. It had been about a month after Christmas when I had invited him over. I still had some mixed nuts in the shells on the coffee table left over from the holidays. Lou sat there and cracked and ate up all of my nuts, which irritated me. Later, he told me that he wanted to make sure that I didn't entertain anyone else with them. Lou was always saying something funny or teasing me. I think that was another thing that drew me to him. After about five or six months of working together, we started dating. I had learned that he had a young daughter that was about the same age as my youngest. The ladies that we worked with had told me that his wife had taken their baby and moved back to Michigan with her mother. Lou never said anything bad about her, but I had heard that she had cheated on him. I tried to get him to tell me about their relationship, but he refused to. In a way I was glad that he wouldn't bad-mouth her, because if anything happened between us, I wouldn't want him talking about me to anyone else. We would go to the movies or take the kids out of town to visit my sister Rita that lived in the Bay Area now. We never had sex although he tried to hold my hand once and I jerked it out of his. I was determined that I was going to live for the Lord. I told him that I didn't want anyone to think badly of me if they saw him holding my hand. I tried to get him to go to church with me, but he wouldn't. When he took me to a movie and a sexual scene came on, I told him that I wanted to leave. I knew that he thought that I was a bit touch in the head, but he stuck with me. We had been dating about eight months when he finally persuaded me to sleep with him. Even though I knew that we should have waited until we were married, I was happy that I had not had sex with him before that. He was the only man that I had ever waited more than one day—two at the most—before we had sex. The Lord was changing me from the inside out. A couple of months after that, he asked me to marry him. I also finally persuaded him to attend church with me. When we went, we sat and listened to the same old hellfire message that the pastor had been preaching for years. I had not yet learned that it is right believing in God's word that would get me started to doing what is right. The more I believed what God said about me in his word, the more I wanted to live right for him. When I left that night, I determined that I wasn't going to go back. I found another church to attend that wasn't so self-righteous. I was tired of being the one pointed out when others were just as guilty as I. It was probably because I would show him things in the Bible that I didn't agree with him on in God's word. I was learning to study the Bible for myself and not just take what people said. Now that Lou and I had gotten serious about each other, it was time to take him to meet my father. I guess that I still wanted his approval in my life. Just for him to say that I did something right for once in my life. I had taken Drew's dad to meet him once before. I found out that he had gone back to his wife. My dad let me know right away that he was not a good man to marry with no hesitation. I decided that it was time for Lou to meet my dad. I had invited my dad down for Thanksgiving dinner and spend the night with us. After eating, he said that my cooking was good but that I could use some more practice, for me not to think that it was perfect. It would have been nice if he had just left it a being good. After I had worked for six months, I was able to get a new car. It was my very first new car that I purchased on my own. We loaded up the kids and drove up to Red Bluff with all five of us in my little Chevy car. Lou had his own car, but I wanted to show off my new car to my dad. All he said was that since I had to pay for it with my own money, now maybe I would take care of it. I introduced Lou to my dad; they seemed to hit it off right away. Lou was originally from Mississippi, a country boy. My father took him and showed him his half-acre garden and the house next door that he built. He asked Lou if he had any children, and Lou told him that he had one in Michigan. Lou was the only man that my dad felt that I should marry or that he liked other than Eddie. I had a love-hate relationship with my dad at this time. I loved him, but I couldn't stand to be around him more than a day in a year. He still was so negative toward me; he would always compare me to Patsy. Patsy had gotten married, Patsy and her husband had bought a house, and Patsy had a good government job. I could subject myself to only so much of that at a time. Although I found out later that Patsy wasn't his pride and joy either; he eventually sent her to live with one of our aunts in Sacramento. I did honor his opinion though as to which man I should or should not marry. I found that I had no clue as to how to choose a husband. I had bought each of the children's dads to him, except Allen, to see what he thought of them. He would tell me that they were not the marrying kind in so many words. But when he met Lou, he asked me if he had any children and if he paid child support. I had learned that Lou had one daughter by a previous marriage. When I told him yes to both questions, he seemed to be satisfied. He took me aside and gave me the father-daughter talk. What he said was that every day won't be roses, but that we would make it. He should have told me that those roses would have many thorns on them before they were pruned. Lou and I had been dating for about eight months. I was thankful that I had not fallen into having sex with him which allowed us to get to know each other without the pressures of sex. He had shared with me that he had been brought up in church and that he had received Christ as a teenager but had strayed away from the church. When he finally did go to church with me, he said that he didn't like the pastor of the church. He said that he had too much control over the people in it. It opened my eyes more to the things that he was going on in that particular church. Again, I had put all of my money in church and was about to get my utilities turned off. Lou gave me the money to pay for it and said that it was wrong of the pastor of the church to tell us to put all of our money in church and not pay our bills. You would think that I would have had enough sense to know better, but I wanted to please God so much that I thought if I disobeyed what the pastor said that God would be mad with me. He always used his authority over us to have us do what he wanted. We had been given into a building fund for over six years now and nothing had been built or even started. I have since learned to listen for the Holy Spirit speak to my inner-self or the peace of God in my giving. Now even from riding on an air plane to spending money I will inquire of God and wait for a check in my sprit to not do a thing or the peace of God before I go ahead. When Lou's birthday came, I bought him a pocket watch for his birthday; it was something that I knew that he liked. When I gave it to him, he told me to take it back and use the money on my children. To me, that was really special. No one ever really thought about my children; their concern was what they could get from me. I needed to learn to value myself. The little gifts and chump change that other men had given me was to curb their own guilt. Not only did Lou care for me; he was concerned about my children's welfare, and that made all of the difference to me. I know that Lou drank and smoked weed, but I turned a blind eye to it since my dad had said that he was the one. The weekend drinking did bother me, but I thought that I could change him. What I did learn was that if the person that you have intentions of marrying has a fault that you don't want to deal with, you had better wait until they change themselves or find someone else because you cannot change people. They have to want to change. I figured if he would just go to church, he would stop drinking, but he refused to go back to the church that I went to. Around the time that I was thinking about breaking off with Lou because of his drinking and smoking weed, I became ill. As I said the church that I went to was very strict and controlling. The only enjoyment that you got outside of church was eating. I had begun to gain weight and was trying to lose it when I read in a magazine about this woman that had lost a lot of weight purging her food when she ate. You know that we never believe that what happens to someone else will happen to us. I didn't believe that it would hurt me although I had read that some people died from purging. I decided to purge my food; that way, I could still eat the food that was almost my only enjoyment and lose weight. I would just do it for a little while. As I said, sin would take you farther than you want to go. Every time that I ate, I would go hide out in the bathroom and vomit my food back up. I began to lose weight—first a half-pound a day then it went to a pound a day. People started to say that I looked sick and that I should stop losing weight. When I looked at myself in the mirror, I still saw myself as fat. After about two months of purging, I began to get acute indigestion, so I decided to stop purging.

When I ate food, it would automatically come back up. I didn't have to make myself throw up anymore. I would get so sick and be in so much pain whenever I tried to eat anything. Finally, I went to the doctor. After running test, they told me that my gallbladder was on the verge of erupting. They wanted to keep me in the hospital and do surgery immediately. My children were at school and I had no one to watch them for me. I know that my godmother would though if I asked her, but Lou said that he was going to watch them and got the key from me to get in. Lou brought some of his clothes to the apartment and stayed in my room while I was in the hospital. He fed and sent my children to school. My godmother would come pick up our dirty clothes and check on the children. She didn't like Lou. Later she told me that she was afraid that he would mess with one of the kids. Later, they fell in love with him; sometimes I think they liked him better than they did me, but that was a good thing. Once, a pair of his underwear got into the wash, and my godmother said that she wasn't washing for him.

When I got out of the hospital, Lou continued to stay there and take care of the children and me. When I was well enough for him to leave, he said that he wasn't going to leave me alone. He slept on one side of the bed and I one the other; of course that did not last long before we started having sexual encounters. I told Lou that I couldn't live with him like that because I was a Christian, but we continued to live together for a while without being married. I felt so guilty about what kind of example that I was being to my children.

One day he and I were going to his place to pick up some of his things; on the way there, he turned to me and said, "Motorcycle mama, will you marry me?" I told him to quit playing around. Lou was always joking about something. Once he asked me if I would take a bite of his purple rock, a phrase from a Hendrix song. After he parked his car in front of his place, he turned in his seat and looked straight into my eyes and said that he wasn't playing. I believed that he was a good man and wouldn't hurt my children. Besides, I had told him in no uncertain words that I would kill him if he ever touched one of my children in the wrong way. He asked me to marry him this time in a more traditional way, and I accepted. Lou had met my pastor the time that he went to church with me. He had listened to him preach before when he had gone with Dot and myself the first time that I met him. When I told the pastor that Lou and I wanted to get married, he said that I shouldn't marry him. He told me that Lou would put a stake in my coffin. I have no idea why he said what he did, but I believed that it was time for me to leave his church. He wanted to control the people too much. After a few months of visiting a few churches, I found one that ministered the word with more understanding. They also believed that God wanted you to prosper in accordance to His word. They said that their ministry had been formed to help Christians that had previously been hurt by other ministers. I enjoyed the word and grew spiritually. Lou would come with me occasionally, but he refused to join. After his divorce was finalized, we decided to purchase a house first before we got married. Lou's credit was pretty bad because he had been moving from place to place and not having his mail forwarded to get his bills. We had decided not to have a big wedding but to just get married at the courthouse and have a reception at the house to save money. With buying a house, paying child support, and raising three children, it would not allow for a large wedding. We planned our marriage for the month of June. I was so happy that my dreams were finally going to be realized and that my dad would finally be happy with me—because I was doing what he asked me to do. He had said that he wanted my sister and me to each be married and buy a house before he died. He told me that he would give us the down payment to put on the house, the same way that he had for my sister and her husband. He was supposed to come down the next week to see the house.

But as life would have it, I was at work a few days before we were to getting married when my Aunt Sherry came to the door in the dietary department. I was surprised to see her and just thought that she had stopped by for a quick visit because she was in the area, not thinking that she would have had a good reason to have been brought to the dietary area where food was being prepared. Aunt Sherry asked me to step outside of the door. When I came out, she told me that she had some bad news to tell me. She said that my father had passed. I was sad and disappointed; sad because I really did love my dad, disappointed because now I could never get his approval on my life. I had done what he asked and now he wouldn't even be around to see that I was going to be somebody worth loving. My dad had told us that he wanted to be cremated, so my sister Patsy and I had his body cremated. My sister Patsy and her husband, Lou and myself drove back up to Red Bluff and had a private memorial service for him. We sprinkled his ashes into the river and let them flow out to sea. He had always said that he wanted to travel. I know that he is not there; it is just the residue from his outward shell. My dad is in heaven now, and when we are reunited, he will be proud of me and we will both have love one to another in the presence of God. We went ahead and signed the papers for our house about a week before we were to get married. Somehow God provided us with the money for the down payment. We had a lovely reception at the house that we just moved into, and my heart dropped on the second night of my marriage. I had never seen Lou sloppy drunk before. We got married on Friday at the courthouse with a mutual friend as a witness and decided to have the reception on the following Saturday evening. Lou celebrated so much that by the time everyone left, he was in the bathroom throwing up. I was afraid that I had made the biggest mistake of my life. I didn't know if I should have the marriage annulled or stick it out.

With Lou working two jobs, we didn't see each other much. We both went to work early shifts; then when we came home, I made dinner and he went to bed before getting up to go to the part-time night job. On weekends, he drank. I would take the kids and go visit my godmother to get away from him. Normally, Lou didn't talk a lot except when he was drinking, then he would talk until he got tired and went to bed. By the time that he went to bed, I was exhausted. With my children and their kid stuff (bickering with one another) and Lou talking nonsense with the drink in him, my life was just an existence except the times that I was at my godmother's. As the children grew into their teen years, they started getting rebellious as most teens do; they would continually get into arguments with each other. It is not always easy to know what to do. My daughter Tee had a sassy mouth, my oldest son was sneaky with his doings, and my youngest was always getting into it with one of the other children's things or smart-mouthing them. At times I put them on restrictions and resorted to the rod of correction. It did help some, but the nitpicking continued. I decided to send them each in turn to live with their dads for a period of time. First, I sent my oldest son to live with his dad Allen, who had moved to Baton Rouge Louisiana. I cried when I took him to the airport; that hurt my heart so much to send him away. I felt that if each one lived for a little while with their dad, then maybe they would appreciate what they had at home. Gerone's dad was very strict, and eventually, Gerone ended up despising his dad. He blames me today for sending him to his dad's. I just pray that he will eventually ask God for help in forgiving his dad. When I sent my daughter to live with her dad, they didn't get along well either. She wanted to go to beautician school and he paid her tuition, but her dad told her that she had to leave, and she lost her money for the school. Of course she held that against me as well. Moms are usually the fall guy for most things. After I left home, my dad gave me a couple of used cars to get around with; because I didn't pay for them, I didn't appreciate them and just drove them until they broke down. It wasn't until I worked and paid for my own car that I finally took care of it. I was determined that I would teach my children how to be responsible adults, so I refused to buy them cars in high school like their friends' parents did. I believed that it would help them be responsible.

I also believed that they should pay a small portion of their paycheck to the house; my belief was that it would prepare them for the world and would teach them to budget their money. Yes, sometimes the extra money that they paid me came in handy; it wasn't always easy trying to feed and clothe a family of five and pay child support. Even if I didn't need the extra money I would have had them pay something anyway because that is what I believed would make them to be a better person. Now that Tee has children I see that she is implementing some of the same things in their lives. When you have children, they will teach you that you are not as perfect as you believe that you are. Although I was the one that was up with my daughter for years when she was a young child and had pains in her navel when her intestines would push out in the hernia until it finally grew in, I was the one that wasn't fair while her dad was somewhere asleep or spending his time with someone else. I was the one that cried and rocked her in my arms until the pain subsided well into the wee hours of the morning. I am also the one that would walk for over a mile just to get to a bus to and from a job. Then I would catch two buses each way to work in the cold and rain because I didn't have a car because I wanted to get off welfare so that they could have a better life. Before I got married, if I asked her dad for something, I had to go to bed with him, even when he was married. The same thing went for my youngest son's dad. Gerone's dad just wasn't there, period. They don't know the junk that I had to go through to make sure that they had nice things like other kids. The thing is that maybe I could have put some money into a bank account for them and gave it to them when they moved to their own places if their dads had been helping out to buy food and clothes instead of using their money on themselves. So this was how I decided to raise my children; now they have decisions to make in raising theirs. Hopefully, some of their decisions will not come back to haunt them, or at least they'll be forgiven for their mistakes. No one is perfect.

CHAPTER

8

I married a man that was willing to take on a wife and three children that were not his. I was still looking for someone to love me for myself. Although Lou drank and smoked weed I was willing to marry him. He was a social alcohol and weed user, but because of my selfrighteous-church upbringing, I couldn't love him as I should have. I was always nagging him to stop drinking and smoking. He was a good man and worked hard to help feed and clothe my children that did not respect him, except for my youngest son. Lou would try to talk to him and do father things with him. He taught him how to drive, but no matter what Lou did, I couldn't appreciate it because of his drinking. It was my husband's drinking that brought me headaches. Lou would drink beer almost every day after we got married, and I detested it. Mostly he would just go to bed after he drank, but sometimes he would try to talk to me or make bad jokes, mostly ones that intimidated me. I had thought that before we got married that I would be able to deal with it. I hated if he wanted to make love after drinking. I detested his friends that would come over and offer him a drink. I started withdrawing from life again except when I would visit my godmother and her family, who for some reason loved him, which made me jealous. Each of my children moved out of the house when they turned eighteen; when my youngest Drew turned seventeen he went to job corps. One weekend when he was supposed to have gone with some of his friends to San Francisco, the police knocked on my door. They said that they were looking for Drew, that he was supposed to have shot someone. I couldn't believe it. Although Drew would bug his sister and brother, he is the kind of person that would give you the shirt off his back if you needed it. After they searched the house, they told me to let them know if he called me. All that I could do was pray and ask God not to let him be killed by them. Too many black sons have been killed by police doing a manhunt for them. During this time with the trial and news media, my husband and my relationship changed. Lou became a rock for me. Yes, we still had a lot—and I do mean a lot—to work out in our marriage; but during this time, I had no one else who even seemed to care or understand except him, and God. During the long process of the trial, my godmother was diagnosed with cancer and was fighting her own battle. After a few months, my godmother passed. Now I didn't have an out. It was like a part of me was missing. My godmother who was a constant in my life was now gone. I had no one to vent to, no one to share with when I was hurting, or encourage me. My sisters and I didn't see each other often. I wasn't used to being around them anymore, and because they weren't living for God, the church that I had gone to had taught me not to associate with them. I didn't believe in getting a divorce unless you were being physically abused. I didn't know that the verbal abuse that my dad had caused me and mental abuse my husband was causing me would be so detrimental to me. I didn't know how to work it out. I didn't know if I could stay with Lou or even if I was willing to as one year turned to another and nothing changed. Because of the sibling rivalry, my other two children were indifferent about their brother. When the other children were dispassionate for me, Lou was there for me. Although my son had a witness that saw him at the time of the shooting, the court convicted him with circumstantial evidence anyway. I had to go to work with this going-on in my son's and my life. I had people at work asking me questions, so-called friends forgetting whom they were talking to and making sarcastic comments about people in jail or prison. I had only God and my husband to turn to for help. Some people wanted to know how I could come to work, but it was as though God gave me wings of eagles to soar over the dark clouds in that time of my life. You hear all of the time of how hard it is to lose a child before a parent. I give God thanks that I have never lost a child to death, but to lose a child to prison I believe to be as bad. I know that when a loved one passes, you will always miss them. It does get better when you understand that you will see them again if you both have died in the Lord. But for the judge to pronounce life without a possibility of parole sentence on an eighteen-year-old child is like a living death. I know that there are some of you who can relate to what I am saying. I am still trusting God that he will return my son to me from the enemy's camp. For years I felt guilty if I enjoyed my life while my son was in prison. I blamed myself for not being a good mother and taking time to be with my children more. I would be so tired and despondent when I came home from work that after I cooked, I would fall asleep on the couch. There were times that I would allow depression to come on me and I would lie on the couch and hope that God would just let me die. Eventually, we bought another house and moved from the neighborhood. I tried to make friends and do things that would take my mind off my son. I became a foster parent, hoping to help someone else's child to go in the right direction in life. I started going out to clubs, so-called lounges with the one friend that seemed to stick with us after my son went to prison because I was so desperate for friendships. I wouldn't allow myself to admit that I was going to a club, but that is what it was all the same. My conscience condemned me, but I told myself that it wasn't wrong. Just before I started going back to the clubs with my friend, God had begun to use me to speak at a couple of church groups into some people's lives. I felt so guilty now that I didn't feel good about telling anyone about God, and the friend that I went to these lounges with would tell me about another minister that would go out to clubs and put him down. I was sure that she did the same to me when I wasn't around. How could I continue to speak to anyone about God with this kind of condemnation? If she talked about him, I was sure that she talked about me too. After a year or so, my faith became weakened. I finally told my friend that I wouldn't be going to any more clubs with her, and I had begun praying again, trying to seek God again, to grow in my faith. But it was not an easy road. One morning, I was on my knees praying and the Holy Spirit told me to pray, saying, "My children shall live and shall not die." I prayed it a couple of times and then stopped, but the Holy Spirit had me to continue praying that my children shall live and shall not die for a few minutes longer. After I felt a release from Holy Spirit, I got up and got dressed for work. A few hours after I began work, I received a phone call that my eldest son Gerone was in the hospital; he had tried to commit suicide. I know now that it was because of God's love for my son and for me that He had me praying for my children. The doctors said that if it had been just a couple of minutes more getting him to the hospital that he would have been dead. At the time, I couldn't see God's mercy that was keeping death back from my children, I could only see that bad things were happening to me. I became so fearful that he would try it again and succeed that I wanted to know where Gerone was every minute. I got him to move in with us so that he wouldn't be alone. Later Gerone, told me that he had been so depressed because of the tinnitus, or ringing in his ears from the loss of hearing, together with sinus problems that was making him so nauseated and dizzy that he didn't want to live like that. God help me; I didn't know that he was depressed. I should have known, I told myself. More guilt, more depression, and fear took hold of my life. Faith, what was that? Some word that I had heard in passing? "My God, my God, why have you forsaken me?" Words uttered by my savior before I was born. He had to go through that feeling on the cross for us when he took on our sin in His body so that we would not be forsaken by the Father in our darkest hour. God was there all the time. He promised that He would never leave us or forsake us. He will never leave us alone, no never. If we can just find a glimmer of a string of hope to hold on to, God will help us. He does not take away the trial that causes us to grow, but we need to look back to the last trial that He brought us through to know that He will bring us through this present one just as he brought us through the one before. When we have done all to stand, stand therefore. In the book of Ephesians, it says, "For we wrestle not against flesh and blood, but against principalities, against powers, against the rulers of the darkness of this world, against spiritual wickedness in high places. Wherefore take unto you the whole armor of God that you may be able to wrestle in the evil day, and having done all to stand. Stand therefore, having your loins girded about with truth, and having on the breastplate of righteousness." If we don't read the word of God, we won't know how to fight the enemy. God's word teaches us how to war against Satan and not people. If we could understand that it is Satan who is the one that comes to steal, kill, and destroy our lives, and that it is Christ Jesus that came to give us life and life more abundantly to the full and overflowing. If we could just understand how much God loves us that He gave His only son to die for us. If we could only fathom the love that God really has for us, we would gladly serve Him out of love and not duty. There was a time in my saved life—yes, saved, sanctified and filled with the Holy Spirit—that I wanted people to get saved so that they can be as miserable as I was. Now God has given me insight and understanding that He is the one that loves us. He is the one that is fighting for us and causes His ministering angels to protect, preserve, and defend us even when we are yet enemies against Him. I pray for sinner's salvation now because I have seen His love in action. I understand that it is Satan who wants to destroy my life along with anyone else's, and it is God who is wrestling for me, trying to woo us into His kingdom just as He is wrestling for you. Satan comes in all forms—mentally, physically, socially, financially, and spiritually—to try to deceive us into believing that God doesn't want us to have a good life. Several months later, Gerone found a doctor that operated on his sinus cavity, and he is much better now. God blessed him and he has bought a nice home for himself and his two dogs. I continue to pray for him because he hasn't yet learned how much God loves him. What I have since learned though was to give Gerone, and the rest of our children, to God to protect. If I was standing next to each and every one of my children, I couldn't save them if it was their time to leave this world. But God can save them if they were halfway across the world if He was not ready for them to go home yet. I needed to cast my cares on God because He cares for me. God can be trusted. Where I had the faith to believe and trust God for the house we wanted—with its six bedrooms on three and one-half acres of land—now I barely found the faith to continue in church fellowship. I was trying to please my friend that I had so desperately wanted after my godmother had passed. I was lonely, I didn't have anyone to talk to, and I was depressed about my son being in prison. I barely saw Lou because now he was working graveyard for the State, and he had started his own lawn service business in the day. My attitude at work went downhill. I developed carpal tunnel syndrome and was let go at work. I couldn't get on to disability because I had not worked for the state long enough so I had no income. I received a disability settlement that was gone in a few weeks, and making payments on the house was becoming a hardship. I would pray, but it seemed as though my prayers would just hit the ceiling of the house and just stop there. My faith to trust God was all but gone. I didn't lose my house I lost my way. There were times that I would get depressed and again I found myself lying on the couch, hoping that God would just let me die. After being in my dream home for four years, we had to sell it and move to a smaller house. My relationship with my other two children was not the best. I only saw my oldest son maybe once a month; after he moved back out on his own again; my daughter had her own life. I saw my daughter when I babysat my grandson, and my youngest son had been moved out of town to a prison. To be honest, at this point in my life, I didn't feel much like living; and I didn't think that Lou would miss me. "The righteous falls seven times, but the Lord will lift him up." Sometimes in the course of our lives Satan will tempt us and we will fall, but don't beat yourself up. Look to the hills from whence comes your help. We put our house up for sale. When we sold our home, we lost about twenty-five thousand dollars on the house, and were charged an early payoff fee. We were able to find a nice three-bedroom home in a decent area and packed up to move. The house we were selling and the one that we were buying were supposed to close on the same day, a Friday in June. When we went to pick up the key so that we could move in, we were told that the one we were moving into hadn't closed, which left us homeless. All of our furniture and clothes were on a large rented truck, and we had nowhere to go. Our faith was being tested. We had to get a motel and wait until the following Monday before we could move in. After we settled into the new house, the Holy Spirit spoke to me to write to the head of the loan company that we had the house through that we had sold and asked for our money back from the early payoff. I explained to them that we could have just walked off and left the house to vandals instead of sticking it out and selling it so that they could be paid. The CEO of the company sent us a check for over seven thousand dollars back. With the extra money, my husband and I were able to go on vacation, something that we had much needed for a while. I did continue to go to church and hear the word. Sometimes when they were praising the Lord with lifted hands, I too would lift my hands and praise God. I would have tears streaming down my face. I am sure that most people probably thought that I was crying because God was ministering to me. But I was crying because I was so depressed and feeling sorry for myself. I couldn't find a job because of the carpal tunnel and tendonitis in my wrists and hands. I am thankful that we were able to buy a house with my husband's salary alone. I decided to be an entrepreneur doing a variety of small businesses of my own. I had heard that if you are going to start a business of your own that you should do something that you enjoy. I should have listened. The first business that I started was cleaning house for disabled people, which didn't last long. I ended up trying to get my husband to help me because I hated it so much. I do well trying to keep my own house clean. After that, I did ceramics tiles that I painted and designed. That was enjoyable, and it brought in money when we needed extra; it lasted for about a year. After that I started painting pictures. I had always loved to paint and draw pictures, so I tried my hand at painting. Through prayer and trusting God, I slowly began to enjoy my life again. I was able to sell some of my paintings at shows that I went to, and that helped for a while. Still, I needed a steady income. The Lord blessed me to get on at Apple computer company. That was a job that I hated from the first hour until the day that my one-year term ended when I walked out of the door at the end. However, this job was one that God used to strengthen my faith and confidence in Him. I had to trust God to help me get through the tests that they gave me, and after that, I needed to get high sales because I didn't know what kind of job that I could get with the carpal tunnel and tendentious. If I had good sales at the end of the year, I could be picked up as a permanent employee, but I couldn't see myself working there any longer. By the end of the year, I had won two monetary awards and could have gotten on full-time, but I decided to use my faith to get back into the state department, which God blessed me to do and from which I am retiring from. I am believing the Holy Spirit to direct me into whatever door God has waiting for me now. God has, and is, blessing my husband and myself more and more as we both grow together in Him. Holy Spirit directed me to another church that now Lou and myself attend. Lou goes with me most every week now; he even watches some programs with me on TV that have great ministers that teach on God's grace.

Now I know that God loves me just because He is *love,* and love is what love does; not because I do everything right or not, but because I don't and can't do everything perfect. Something that really helped me to understand God's love for me was when he let me know that He was and is now concerned about every little thing in our lives no matter how big of how small. One weekend we were traveling upstate to visit my youngest son in prison when the Holy Spirit spoke into my spirit to bring my camera as I was packing for the trip. I listed to myself reasons why I shouldn't bring it with us. I knew that we couldn't take pictures at the prison, and I had been through the mountains of Nevada and had taken pictures before, so I decided that I didn't need it. Again just before we left, He again urged me to bring the camera; again, I reasoned why I shouldn't. When we got to Reno, they were having a hot air balloon event. God the Father knew that I love to see hot air balloons. He loves me so much that He wanted me to be able to not only enjoy the event but to have pictures to enjoy later. Because I didn't have my camera with me, I had to go find a store that sold disposable cameras to take pictures. When we first arrived at the balloon event, they were still on the ground, by the time we got back, they were in the air, some too far to get good pictures. If I had listened, not only would I have gotten good pictures of the balloons on the ground, I would also have gotten great pictures of them when they first were airborne. There were so many different kinds: cows, Disney cartoon caricatures, striped, and polka dot. I am learning to not question the Holy Spirit and just obey. The Holy Spirit will never lead us to do anything that will harm us, only bless our lives and make it richer. Through this incident and many others, God has shown me how much He really loves me. I have learned to value myself by what God says that I am and not what man says I am. The book of Ephesians also says, "And may you have the power to understand, as all God's people should, how wide, how long, how high, and how deep His love is." May you experience the love of Christ, though it is too great to understand fully. Then you will be made complete with all the fullness of life and power that comes from God. I am confident that God will grow us both in him. We have a much better relationship since I am following the Holy Spirit's guidance more, even when Holy Spirit tells me to be quiet. My husband has been a rock to me since my youngest son has been in prison and encourages me when the other children are doing their own thing. I know that he loves me and we both need each other. We have both gone through hard lives, with Lou being separated from his mother and siblings as a young child. Now we are strength to each other through Christ. We both tease and play with each other and have fun together. I am not as touchy, defensive, and self-righteous as I once was. As we both grow in the word, we have come to appreciate each other's strengths and weaknesses.

We both laugh at ourselves when we think of some of the strange things we get into. We both love to travel and fish. One day we were looking for the travel park where we were supposed to meet one of my sisters at. We went around the place and passed it and almost through the place without knowing it. When we stopped to ask for directions. The lady told us to go back the way we came and to go back under the bridge and turn at an orange tree by a saloon. We promptly told her that we hadn't gone under a bridge to get where we were.

Nevertheless, we obediently went back the way we had come. To our amazement, we had passed under a bridge and had both missed it. And at the corner of the saloon, there sat the orange tree, a fruit tree; we had thought it was going to be a tree that was colored orange with some attachment to the saloon. We both still laugh at our plights that we encounter. God is blessing us more and more as we allow Him to have more control of our lives. I would do you an injustice if I didn't tell you this last thing. With all of the rapes, sexual perversion, and being put down in my lifetime, I couldn't understand what people found so attractive about having sex. Having a sexual encounter with any man including my husband brought me no pleasure. Sometimes I would go into the bathroom and change into my pajamas or wait until he left the room so that my husband wouldn't see me naked and want to have sex. I was always glad when it was over; most of the time I would think of something else and fake my pleasure in it or watch TV if it was on when we were in the act. What I want you to know is that there is life and love after being raped and molested. After I had been married about ten years, my husband and I were at home alone relaxing. We were stress free for a little while with no children around and we decided, or he decided, that he wanted to make love. He began with the foreplay ritual as usual. I can't tell you what was different about this time, but I began to respond to him, and the next thing I knew was that I didn't know what was happening to me. I didn't know if I had died and gone to heaven or if I had gone to Mars, but if heaven is half as sweet, then I don't want to miss it. I know that God is still healing me in areas of my life, but He wanted you to know that he is the author of love. When we get into the word of God and learn what he says about us and what His will for us is, we can leave the cares and depressions of the world behind us. Isaiah 60:1 says, "Arise from the depression and prostration in which circumstances have kept you, rise to a new life; Shine with the glory of the Lord, for your light has come, and the glory of the Lord has risen upon you!" If you have not yet asked Christ to come into your life and change your life for the good, please don't let another day go by, ask Jesus into your life now. Now that I have the rest of my life to learn how to have loving relationships with Jesus, Holy Spirit, and Daddy God, I have a life worth living. Now through good Christian teaching, I have learned that you should interact with your children and listen to their disagreements to your rules. It doesn't mean that you will always change your decision, but at least think about it and weigh out what they are saying. God could just be speaking through them. I have also learned because bad things happen to us that we don't have to continue to make bad decisions and choices. It is about doing good to one another, letting God's love through you. It is honoring one another. By the grace of God, I have a great relationship with my children and my husband now. I am still standing in faith for my youngest son to come home from prison. You see, nothing is too hard for God. In God's word, He says, "And they shall be Mine, says the Lord of hosts, in that day when I publicly recognize and openly declare them to be My jewels, My special possession, My peculiar treasure." You may have once been man's trash, but you can be God's treasure. Have you ever really wanted to do something nice for someone or to give them a gift? One morning, God showed me what it was like for Him to want to give us a special gift and have us try to buy it from him after he went through all of the sacrifice and trouble of providing it for us. I had told my sister about a special dish that I made. We are always trying to eat healthy and keep our weight down, so I came up with this really great stew that I called fish stew. It is almost like a seafood gumbo but without the crab, but still very expensive. Good fish is almost as expensive as crab here in northern California. I went to the store and bought all of the ingredients. I took my time and was very careful to add the right amount of each seasoning. I made sure that each of the items that went into it was added just so, checked the flavors and cooked it until it got to perfection. I called my sister to come over to try it. After she tasted it, she said that she really enjoyed it and would like some. I gave her a nice helping in a container to take with her for her and her husband to share. What she did next was almost like throwing it back into my face. She took out a twenty-dollar bill and told me to not say a word and just take it. I made the stew from my heart and wanted to share it with her because I knew that it would be good for her. I was willing to give her the recipe for the stew that would be beneficial to her losing and keeping off weight in her future. All she had to do was receive it. Giving me the money was like her saying I helped to pay for it, that it's not really a gift. God provided His son Jesus to hang on the cross for our sins. He was the only one who was able to keep the entire law without sin. God has provided everything for us; we just have to receive it. We receive God's gift, Jesus Christ and the Holy Spirit, by faith, not by works or payment trying to help pay for our salvation by working to obey the law instead of being led by the Spirit of God knowing that Jesus has done everything. If we could pay for our sins, then Christ died in vain. We are to just rest in His finished work and follow the directions of Holy Spirit as He guides us. Right believing in God's word will lead you to right doing, and God will love you until you get there. If you believe that He really loves you, you will want to do what is pleasing to Him. Say about yourself what He says about you. He gave us his recipe—it is the Bible; try reading it, and you can be a well-rounded cake.

ABOUT THE AUTHOR

Georgia Smith is a graduate of MTI Business School. She is a freelance writer, and painter. Many of her paintings have been copyrighted and have had prints sold. She has spoken to groups of women about the subject of this book, particularly in church groups. She has also spoken to men, and mixed genders in places of business on other subjects.

Georgia was born in a small town in California, and moved to Sacramento California where she met and married her husband of thirty-six years. They have a blended family of four children and seven grandchildren of whom they enjoy as often as possible, especially on holidays, along with their two dogs and six coy and goldfish. She has two sisters, as well as one brother who has moved on with the Lord to better things. She attends a great church of mixed ethnic backgrounds which she loves.